Creative
Storytelling

with Children at Risk

Creative Storytelling

with Children at Risk

Sue Jennings

Speechmark

I dedicate this book with love, and respect, to my friend and colleague
Dr Alida Gersie, who is a never-ending source of inspiration and wisdom.

Cover illustration by Chloe Gerhardt

First published in 2004 by
Speechmark Publishing Ltd, 70 Alston Drive, Bradwell Abbey, Milton Keynes MK13 9HG, UK
Tel: +44(0) 1908 326944   Fax: +44 (0) 1908 326960
www.speechmark.net

Reprinted 2007, 2011

002-4722 Printed in the United Kingdom by CMP (uk) Ltd

British Library Cataloguing in Publication Data
Jennings, Sue
      Creative storytelling with children at risk
      1. Narrative therapy
      2. Child psychotherapy
      I. Title
      618.9'289166

ISBN 978 0 86388 271 5

Contents

Acknowledgements

I WOULD LIKE TO THANK all the children with whom I play and tell stories; my own children and grandchildren; Dan and Luminiţa for all their inspiration; and Suzanne Hall and Chloe Gerhardt for creative ideas and illustrations. A special thank you to Joan Moore for allowing me to include the story of Katie, and her imaginative stories and plays.

CHAPTER 1

Introduction

Stories, Nature, and Play: The Heritage of our Children

THIS BOOK IS ABOUT the ways in which we can tell and create stories with children who are troubled. Stories provide a safe structure both for telling our personal story and for hearing a story that can be helpful to us when we are anxious or burdened. Stories can be told, painted, enacted or shown through the sand tray. The important thing is that the story is communicated and heard: stories are not told in order for adults to pick over the bones of children and derive conclusions about them. Adults may understand children and their needs more when children are able to create and tell stories, but the most important thing is the telling and the hearing. Out of the stories can come plans, changes, and variations, so that we can feel more empowered to take action and to ask for help. Sometimes the externalising of the story can, in itself, bring about understanding and a lightening of the burden.

Perhaps we can remember that next time we 'have a good gossip' with a friend or colleague, we are usually telling a story in order to get something off our chest, or in an attempt to understand someone else – unless we are gossiping about Royalty and famous people, when we may be expressing the new myths and fairy stories that belong to this generation. I am not, of course, including malicious gossip that is inappropriate for our purpose, and can result in a depersonalising 'tabloid' approach to people. However, healthy gossiping is oral storytelling, and an important part of our communication.

Play and stories are essential to the development of healthy children, but we sometimes forget that children need to be able to play out of doors. For many children, their first encounter with the 'big wide world' is when they toddle outside in the garden or the park. However much we re-create outdoors indoors, through sand and water play, wild animals, or by having nature murals on the walls, and animals in bowls and cages, it cannot match the real experience of being outside. We can tell story after story about the world outside, but it does not replace the exploration of outdoors, or the uniqueness of telling stories outside. I visited a nursery once where they had plastic grass for an indoor lawn. Outdoor play and adventures are essential to a child's development at several different levels, and this is an issue that needs to be addressed in planning, building and all kinds of educational provision. Many playing fields have been sold off for development, and I am sure that this fact is not unrelated to the very high proportion of inactive, obese children and adults that currently cause concern to health practitioners.

Infants and children need to come into contact with the natural world as early in their lives as possible. I know this is not easy for people in inner-city settings, but it is possible. Nurseries and playgroups can have outings, whatever the weather, even as far as the local park or nearby beach. I am sure we can all remember the sheer delight of puddle-jumping and splashing, laughing as the wind blew us along, and making caves and creating castles with seaside sand, shells, and stones.

The outdoor world is one of extremes for young children: it is either much larger than they are, and they gaze at enormous trees, animals, and the expanse of sky; or it is infinitely smaller than they are, and their sharp eyes see ladybirds, ants, and spiders in all their minute detail.

It is important for children to learn about the four seasons and the four elements. Being aware of the seasons and the passing of the year creates the cycle of nature, together with the celebrations that go with the seasons. With the advent of the freezer, it is less easy to be aware of the seasons through the fruit and vegetables we use, because we are not reliant on things being 'in season'. It is less usual now for us to preserve and store things for the winter, and the rituals surrounding the making of seasonal food – for example, the mixing of the Christmas puddings once autumn is here, the harvesting of fruits for making jam in certain months, and the cutting and boiling of the ingredients for chutney and pickles – happen less and less. Children can become involved in the harvesting and preparation of fresh produce, and feel part of the cycle of nature.

The four elements are an important part of a child's experience, and we can see children responding to them in quite a primitive way. They run and scream as the wind carries them along; they love getting wet in rain and running water; they feel supported by the earth, and explore it in many ways; they are kept warm by fire, and view it with a mixture of awe and fascination. Air, water, earth, and fire can also be associated with the seasons, and we can observe how the different elements change with the seasons.

By experiencing the natural world, in so far as it is still natural, children become aware of the environment. They begin to understand the importance of the environment around them, not only animals in distant places. A child then develops a sense of his or her place in the story of the natural world, as a part of the whole, rather than someone who will be in control. Indeed, some of the magnificence is the enormity of the world around us: the carpet of stars on a clear night, and the resounding thunderstorm. Apart from organised sports and games, it is healthy for children to be able to create their own play

in nature and even in the wild: it serves to stimulate and stretch the imagination. However, it is also important that children learn to care for the environment in their play early on.

We must not neglect the older child and adolescent in this context. Children who have learned to respect the environment, experienced the security of story structures, and learned through developmental play, are unlikely to destroy and vandalise their surroundings. The great challenge is to find ways for them to re-experience the great outdoors, rather than locking them in boot camps. Unfortunately, this is a view that does not win votes or media popularity.

All these experiences in the great outdoors can form a backdrop to our storytelling, as well as enabling children and adolescents themselves to create stories. Stories can be told or enacted, drawn or modelled, or read from the great story books. The outside world can be a challenge as well as an inspiration, so we need to belong to it while it still exists.

Sue Jennings
Glastonbury 2004

CHAPTER 2

The Story of Stories

Introduction

THIS CHAPTER DESCRIBES THE background to storywork, and my own particular philosophy of 'Nature – Theatre – Play'. We consider children's rights to their own art and culture, which are now enshrined in law. I emphasise the importance of the balance between our concerns and the resources available, and suggest ways in which we can monitor this balance, both for ourselves and the child. The importance of social play as well as personal play is suggested as an integrated approach. The chapter ends with guidance on how to use this book, and suggestions for personal and professional record keeping.

Background

When I ponder the creation of this book, I realise that I am moving on from my previous writings. During the 1980s and 1990s I published a number of books specifically about dramatherapy and playtherapy. They serve their purpose, and present theory and practice from myself, and many colleagues, to a wide audience of professional therapists and educators. However, I feel that it is important to step back a few paces: for me, it is important to work with the bigger picture, the bigger story, the bigger stages, and to go beyond the limitations of something we choose, in the Western world, to name 'therapy'. My basic philosophy is Nature – Theatre – Play, and the connection between them. Of course one thing connects all three and that is stories. There are nature stories; the theatre dramatises stories; and, in play, we are always creating stories. Nature and theatre create a perfect balance – a balance between nature and culture.

Stories, and their dramatisation through play, are at the core of human happiness and the continuing development of children, young people, and adults. Indeed, they are universally important for the health and welfare of all children. This belief is enshrined in the Convention on the Rights of the Child, which was adopted by the General Assembly of the United Nations (1989):

- Parties recognise the right of the child to rest and leisure, and recreational activities appropriate to the age of the child, and to participate freely in cultural life and the arts.
- Parties shall respect and promote the right of the child to participate fully in cultural and artistic life, and shall encourage the provision of appropriate and equal opportunities for cultural, artistic, recreational, and leisure activity.

It is important to note that the Convention emphasises the artistic and cultural life of children. Drama, stories, and theatre are part of children's rights, which leads me into my wider perspective. I wanted to write a book to reflect the bigger story, to enable all those people who work with children, both their own and other people's, to re-connect with this vital source of pleasure, transformation, and energy. I hope that the pathways I suggest will enable you, the reader, to refresh your existing expertise, to discover new ideas and ways of making stories and playing and dramatising them.

Does the Task Seem too Great?

Why do we still find areas of education and care where the importance of stories is not recognised, and where play is seen as a luxury? Alternatively, we find that stories and play are corrupted and distorted by people who abuse children, and phrases such as 'special time', 'special story', or 'special friend' become part of a beguiling technique for enticing young children. We have to find new words and phrases to create the inspiration of storytelling and the magic of play. It is easy to become daunted if we can only see how enormous the difficulties are when working with children at risk: developing suitable structures for storytelling and play may seem an impossible challenge.

We can make our contribution in our own way, and can make our mark, but we cannot influence everything that is unjust towards children. We can find our own voice and make sure that it is always heard. Or does that feel too big a task?

Techniques to Support Us

My friend Linda reminds me that we need to keep our circles of influence and concern in proportion to each other: we must not allow our enormous circle of concern to grow bigger than our circle of possible influence, or else we will do nothing effectively, because there will not be enough energy in our resources. Although people will say, 'If you want to get something done, then ask a busy person', we need to resist the flattery! We need to practise the skill of saying 'No'. We can apply this philosophy to our work with children. For example, the child's circle of hurt needs to be balanced with the child's circle of care; and, similarly, our own circle of care needs to be in proportion to our own hurts and wounds. Maybe we need to increase our own circle of care.

It is a useful exercise to complete Worksheet 1: Circles of Concern and Influence. In the first circle, 'My Circle of Concern', write all the things that you have concerns about – examples may include personal and health issues; the family; the community; your work; global issues, and disadvantage. I am sure you can find many more. In the second circle, 'My Circle of Influence',write the many different ways in which you have influence – examples may include your knowledge-base about personal and family concerns, your doctor, the library, or the internet; your skills at dealing with the family, or listening to advice from others; and your interest in volunteering for a project, or becoming involved in community matters. As you elaborate on the two circles, you will find that certain things will match and balance, but there are usually a lot of issues left over. For example, you may feel you should take on all the issues concerning the children with whom you work, become involved in every community project, give to all the charity and disaster appeals, and worry about all the injustice in the world. Now is the time for re-appraisal: you need to decide on what is possible. Obviously immediate personal, family, and work issues have to be addressed; however, sometimes we can have a fresh perspective on these if we do something else that is completely different. For example, when I went to work in a Romanian hospital for long-stay psychiatric patients who often did not have enough to eat, I gained a fresh perspective on my criticisms of my hospital work in the UK. Similarly, if we feel very strongly about nature and the environment, perhaps we can do a course that enables us to speak with authority on the subject – there are many colleges and universities that provide such training.

These circles of concern and influence give us the chance to create a balance in our concerns and our capacity to influence those concerns, and enable us to make decisions about the best way forward. They certainly help us to address the feelings of being overwhelmed by so much need in the world.

Worksheet 1
Circles of Concern and Influence

Name _____ Date _____

My Circle of Concern

My Circle of Influence

Is the Child Feeling Overwhelmed?

We can use a variation on the two circles as an assessment method for working with children. One circle will be for listing the needs of the child and our concerns about the child, the other circle will be for identifying the resources (or potential resources) available for the child. Are we trying to provide all the resources ourselves? Other people need to be involved: statutory bodies, teachers, mentors, supervisors, and colleagues. We can then re-appraise our circle, and create another circle that includes the skills and knowledge-base of others.

The two circles in Worksheets 1 and 2, the two bags (Worksheet 3), or the weighing scales (Worksheet 4), can be used with children who seem burdened. They are similar to the Mandala technique described in Chapter 7: Stories for Feelings and Emotions. You can invite a child to fill in the two circles in Worksheet 2, 'Things that worry me' and 'Things that help me', or 'My bag of worries' and 'My bag of good things' in Worksheet 3. When using Worksheet 4, you can have an actual pair of weighing scales and small objects for the child to place on them. The objects on one side represent worries, and objects on the other side represent things that are helpful. The aim is to see if they can be balanced. The child does not have to do this alone: you and the other responsible adults in the child's life are a part of the picture.

It may be that the hurt cannot be balanced, and that there is very little in the positive bag or on the positive side of the weighing scales. Many of the children with whom we work have things loaded very much against them. It will make a difference if we can build up a relationship of trust and respect through the story and play work that we do. We need to search for stories that contain some hope for the future. A good example of a story created for a child when hope is needed is described in Chapter 8: The Child's Story. The following story, 'The Bunny who thought she was a Porcupine', was created by a colleague for a child with very low self-esteem.

Worksheet 2
Things that Worry Me/Things that Help Me

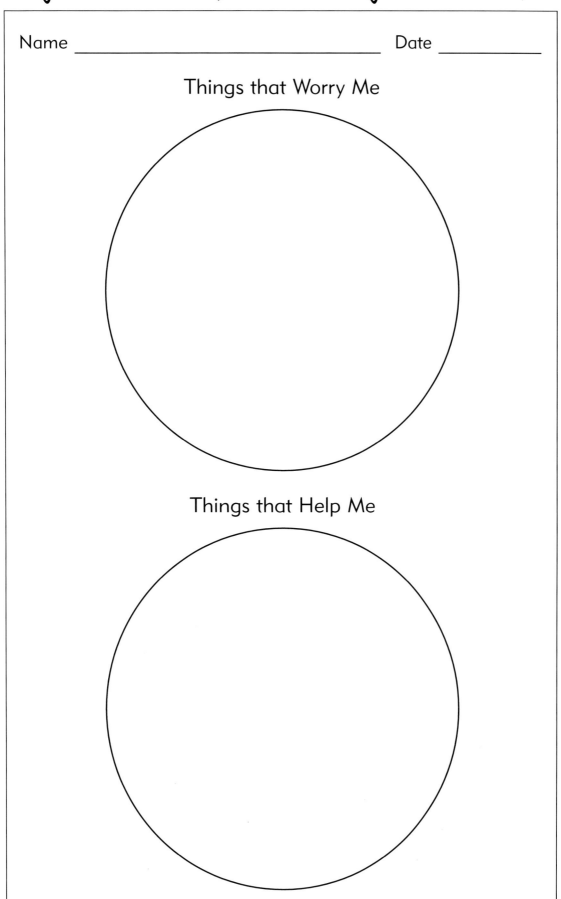

Name _____ Date _____

Things that Worry Me

Things that Help Me

Worksheet 3
The Two Bags

Name _____ Date _____

My Bag of Worries

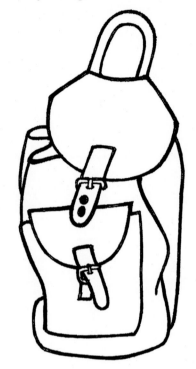

My Bag of Good Things

Worksheet 4
Weighing Scales

Name _____ Date _____

Things that Worry Me

Things that Help Me

_____   _____
_____   _____
_____   _____
_____   _____
_____   _____
_____   _____
_____   _____

The Bunny who thought she was a Porcupine

Once upon a time, in a tiny copse deep in the countryside, a very pretty bunny was born. The bunny had the softest velvet eyes and the fluffiest fur you could imagine. Sadly, the bunny's mum had a disease in her eyes that prevented her from being able to see how pretty her youngest bunny was. This disease made the Mummy Bunny very bad-tempered. She frequently screamed at her youngsters, who found it hard to please her. She especially picked on her youngest bunny, who was least able to look after herself, so grew up believing that she must be nasty and ugly because Mummy Bunny told her so. The other bunnies in the family sided with their mother as it was safer to keep in with her. They teased, told tales on, and fought with their little sister, until her beautiful soft fur became matted with sores from prickly burrs and thorns. The other animals became worried, and told Wise Owl; so the pretty bunny was taken to live with a family of badgers who were kind to her.

Bunny felt happier living in the badgers' set. She admired their striking colouring that gave them a sleek appearance, and she wished that she could be like them. One day she looked into a pond, to see how she might change to be more like them. There were lots of reeds behind the bunny as she looked into the pond. They made her reflection look like a porcupine. Suddenly, the little bunny thought she saw why her first family had been so nasty to her. 'So, I'm a porcupine!' she said to herself. 'It's no wonder no one likes me! I'm ugly and prickly, and no one wants to come near me.' She sat down, and cried, and cried, and cried. Just then a butterfly fluttered by, and landed on a nearby leaf when she heard the bunny's distress. 'Hello Bunny', she said. 'Why is such a pretty bunny as you feeling so unhappy?' 'You must be crazy!' said Bunny, a bit rudely, but feeling quite desperate by now. 'Surely you can see I'm not a bunny, just a porcupine full of ugly spikes!' 'What makes you think that?' enquired the butterfly. 'You look like a bunny to me, and a very pretty one too!' Bunny smiled at the butterfly. 'Thank you', she said, though she still found it hard to believe. Bunny confessed that she didn't think anyone liked her. She had too many prickles that felt stuck too close to her heart. The butterfly told Bunny that she was soft and beautiful, but needed to find strength inside herself. Then the butterfly picked out all the prickly burrs from Bunny's fur. Bunny felt much happier when she'd finished: she began to bounce and spring on the grass, feeling free of her prickles at last.

Suddenly Bunny stopped springing. 'What if the others don't realise I'm a bunny?' she asked. 'They're used to me being prickly. What shall I do if they carry on being horrid to me?' 'Ah!' said the butterfly, 'You must learn to protect yourself.' 'How?' asked Bunny. 'Well,' said the butterfly, 'If you act like the soft, pretty, kind bunny you are, the animals you want to make friends with will like you – the others aren't worth bothering with. But it's best not to tell the animals about your prickles, or they will think you still have them and they might tease you, without realising that it hurts.'

The butterfly had given Bunny lots to think about. Later, Bunny met Owl, who said that he had found a rabbit that was looking for a bunny to look after. Bunny told Owl about the conversation she had just had with butterfly. The Owl said he thought the butterfly was giving sensible advice.

Bunny moved to live with Rabbit, and discovered life was much calmer: it was nicer being with someone who treated you properly. The prickly burrs disappeared for good as Bunny made lots of friends at her new home with Rabbit.

The Healing of Trees

The Story of the Old Forest does not make any promises: rather, it creates images of containment and care. There are ancient truths in this forest, and beautiful birds and animals who are unafraid. Secrets are protected and wounds can be healed, through the ancient layers of the undergrowth. We explore more images of trees in several of the following chapters.

> Trees create stability through their roots, growth through their trunks, development through their branches, and seeds of new life through their fruits.

The Story of the Old Forest

'In a land far away there is an old, old forest that has been untouched for thousands of years. There is a winding river that flows through the forest and at times disappears in the undergrowth. The trees meet overhead to form a green arch, which creates a shining green tunnel. Forest animals come down to the river bank to drink, unafraid and content. Some ancient trees tower thousands of feet above the undergrowth, and give homes to beautiful birds and tree creatures. The forest has layers and layers of undergrowth which has been growing, layer upon layer, for hundreds of years: it guards ancient secrets, and heals the dark wounds from the past.'

After hearing the Story of the Old Forest one little girl called Sarah created her own version of the story:

> **Sarah's Story**
>
> This is a special sort of magic tree, and the fruit are magic. The tree is in a forest. In the forest lives a badger, a fox, a squirrel, and a bird. In the middle of the tree lives Father Christmas, who will bring me a present.

Caring for the Environment: Nature-Theatre-Play

The Story of the Old Forest also introduces another theme that is dear to my heart: the care of the environment. This is the Nature aspect of the Nature-Theatre-Play philosophy. The natural environment is all we have left that can be permanent in our surroundings, but it continues to be destroyed by pollution and exploitation. The children's immediate surroundings in home and school need to be safe. If we care for the child, we also need to care for the environment, so that the child can feel part of an ethos of concern. When children feel part of the wider universe, of nature and wildlife, they also experience their lives from new perspectives – they are part of the rhythms and seasons of the big world. Thus the child who can feel connected to the Story of the Old Forest may feel some comfort from the repetition of the images and the 'holding' of the wounds.

Many people will recall the controversial book *Silent Spring* by Rachel Carson, published in the 1960s. Carson was the first person to provoke us with ideas about, and the immediacy of, ecology and the environment. For centuries romantic ideas about the pastoral life have been common themes for poets and philosophers alike – the opening lines of Act II of Shakespeare's *As You Like It* are a famous example of the contrast between urban and pastoral living:

> Now, my co-mates and brothers in exile,
> Hath not old custom made this life more sweet
> Than that of painted pomp? Are not these woods
> More free from peril than the envious court?
> *As You Like It* II. i. 1–4

However, it is since the 1960s that there has been an increasingly vocal, proactive movement concerning the environment and our responsibilities towards Green issues. Most local authorities now have an environmental officer, and many schools teach environmental issues in the curriculum. But this does not always seem to connect with the business of living and playing: many children do not have healthy food, that has been produced in a sustainable way, at school or in their snack boxes.

Cooking and Eating Together

Crisp packets and drink cans litter the pavements, and we know that there is a generation of families that has never learned to cook. More and more children are obese or have other forms of eating disorders, and increasing numbers of them are hyperactive. There are two primary social activities that are often missing from children's lives: cooking, and eating together, at least from time to time. These activities can also be mirrored in play activity and storytelling.

In the following tale, Lily tells us a food story which expresses her hopes for a special present.

Mum Saying 'Yuk' to the Potato

Once upon a time there was a little lady called Mum and she tried to eat a potato and thinks 'Yuk' and her sister told her Granny who sent her to bed. Mum cried and cried all day and she never came down to hug her Mummy 'cos she's just a kid called Mum. Mum never came down so she came down in the middle of the night and left some peas and a drink so then she went to her bedroom. So Father Christmas noticed that she was a good little girl and only came to Mum in her bedroom and left her a present – no one else. She opened it and it was a real good puppy. She went to her Mummy to wake her up, then she hit her Mummy to wake her up. Mum telled her about the puppy. Mum was so happy she walked the dog every day, in the evening, in the night and even in the middle of the night.

Many stories and rhymes include the themes of gathering or harvesting fruits or crops, or cooking and eating together. There are seasonal rituals which accompany planting and harvest time, and they vary from culture to culture. Children feel affirmed if we know about their rituals and celebrations, and ask them to tell us more about them. Social rituals create solidarity, and help the child to feel part of the wider group.

The Russian educational theorist, Vygotsky (1978) argued that our personal and social experiences cannot be separated. The world that children inhabit is influenced not only by their families, but also by their communities, education, and culture. Children's understanding of the world comes from the adults and children who people their world. This means that we do not have to place the emphasis solely on the play and story work that we do with children: we can also include the cultural and ritual context that belongs to the child.

> One reason that we tell stories with children is that it expands their world, as well as affirming their social identity and culture.

Children's play often involves scenes of parties and eating, using the dolls' house or the miniature tea-set. In our storytelling and playing, it is crucial that there are human values about respect for the environment and for each other that act as role models for children. 'Setting an example' seems to be a very old-fashioned concept now; but however much we believe in non-directive play in order for a child to express him or herself, it needs to be balanced with structured play and storytelling that give security and confidence.

Being a Storyteller

Part of our task, when we work with children, is to find the story that the child needs to hear: this will sometimes be a story that we have devised for the child, often on the spur of the moment, a task which becomes easier as we practise our storytelling skills. Another part of our task is to have a large repertoire of stories, from many cultures and countries, that we can share with the children when appropriate. The 'given' stories need to be told in a story-telling mode, that is, with us in the role of the storyteller: we need to know how to use our voices to paint pictures with language as we tell these tales.

The stories that we devise, as well as the given stories, provide a safe container for the stories that the child needs to hear from us. Children will often tell their personal stories through puppets or other toys, or through an adaptation of a fairy tale or television drama. Many children will not tell their story until they feel they can trust us, and they know that we listen to them with respect. There is anxiety that no one will listen to their story, or that people will laugh at or reject it. Even then, it is not uncommon for a child to use metaphors and time displacement (a long time in the past or in the future) in order to create safety for the expression of their lives. Children will also use a fairy-tale structure, with archetypal characters and plots, to create stories that they need to tell and enact. The following story was created by an eight-year-old child in care with her play therapist.

The Princess, the Vampire/Jester, and the Bodyguard

Vampire enters, disguised as Court Jester.

VAMPIRE: Good evening Princess: I have come to provide you with some entertainment for the evening. What would you like to see?

PRINCESS: I don't know who you are. *(Whispers to bodyguard.)*

BODYGUARD: Don't trust him your Highness – we don't know who he is. I'll send him packing if you like.

(Bodyguard brandishes sword, and Vampire skulks off. Vampire then returns, dressed as an old lady.)

VAMPIRE: Good evening Princess: I have brought a gift for you. May I come in?

PRINCESS: Oh how nice; do come in. Sit down right here. *(Pats seat next to her.)* Now then, show me what you have brought.

VAMPIRE: Well, first of all, Princess, tell me what secrets you've got. I need to know – as I'm growing old, I might die soon, then it will be too late.

PRINCESS: *(Becoming suspicious.)* I can't tell you that. I don't know who you are. Besides, I don't know if you're good or bad. What have you brought me?

VAMPIRE: I have some pretty things to show you. I just want to be your friend.

PRINCESS: *(To bodyguard.)* What do you think?

BODYGUARD: *(Whispering to Princess.)* Let's see how real she is.

(He and the Princess invent a lie detector, and run it over the 'old lady'.)

BODYGUARD: *(Whispering to Princess).* I think it's the Vampire, your Highness: this old lady is bad. Shall I get rid of her for you?

PRINCESS: Yes, take her away! Get lost, you horrible old woman! *(Starts screaming and waving bells on a stick.)*

VAMPIRE: *(Puts hands over ears.)* Aaah! Stop that screaming! You know I can't bear the screaming! Don't worry, I'm off! I hate those bells! Aaaah!

(Vampire exits, and reappears dressed as a bad fairy.)

VAMPIRE: Hello Princess. I've come to bring you good wishes. What would you like to happen?

(Princess consults bodyguard because she doesn't know what to believe. The bodyguard advises her to be careful.)

VAMPIRE: I have some beautiful jewellery for you, Princess. Shall I show you how well these rings will fit your pretty little fingers? *(Ties ribbon tightly round her finger.)*

PRINCESS: Ouch! You're hurting me! Help! Help!

VAMPIRE: *(Showing his nasty side.)* Ah! I'm really going to get you this time! *(Princess screams.)* Think you can get away from me do you? I'll show you!

(Vampire throws Princess into jail: Princess tries to fight back, and gets thrown back into jail three times.) Princess screams for bodyguard.

BODYGUARD: This time you'll die! *(Sends Vampire packing.)*

(Enter Good Fairy with wand.)

GOOD FAIRY: I'm the Good Fairy, and I'm going to make sure everyone is safe. *(Waves wand and makes a happy spell.)*

Telling My Own Story

In our work with children we will feel touched and troubled from time to time, and it is helpful if we can recall our own experiences from childhood. I suggest that you keep a large notebook in which to record your own stories. As you read *Creative Storytelling with Children at Risk* it will provoke memories and feelings, and even dreams, all of which may contribute to your work. You may like to start with the following reflections, and I also include some of my own.

Think about the games that you played as a child, and the stories that you remember with affection. Were there games that were frightening? Were there stories that you did not want to hear? Remember to write them down in your story-book – can you recall how you overcame these fears as you grew up?

The Princes in the Tower

I was an early reader as a child, and spent a lot of time reading on my own. I still vividly remember reading a very graphic and emotional account of 'The Princes in the Tower' at the age of eight. I sobbed and sobbed, and no one was able to console me for hours – they could not say that it was 'just a story' as it was written in an encyclopaedia! The painting and description haunted me for years.

However, a couple of years later I was given a book called *The Black Riders* by Violet Needham, which tells the story of a boy who lives with his aunt and uncle in a country cottage. I write about it in some detail in the next chapter, and describe the ways in which it became one of my own healing stories.

Think again about the games and stories that you have written down in your story-book, and ask yourself whether any of them have had a healing function for you. Is there a story that you would have liked to be told all those years ago? Is it possible to tell yourself that story now? Write down a poem or story that is important for you, and decorate it if you wish. As we journey through this book we can allow ourselves our own personal journey, which will inform our work as well as ourselves.

Where are the stories we heard as a child? Are we too grown up to recall them?

Where are the stories we loved as a child? Are we too busy to hear them?

Where are the stories we feared as a child? Did the dragons really come true?

Let's tell the stories we loved as a child, and find joy in the telling.

Let's recall the fears, the ghosts and the bears,

And remember we're not always grown-up.

CHAPTER 3

How to Find this Book Useful

Introduction

IN THIS CHAPTER WE look at the practicalities of storytelling with children. There are six questions to ask: 'Who?', 'What?', 'Why?', 'When?', 'Where?', and 'How?' These questions need to be asked several times in order to really understand what we might create with the children we work with, as well as with ourselves. They are also very useful in focussing work as well as aiding clarity in evaluation and assessment. They were originally suggested in 1974 by Viola Spolin, in her extraordinary book about teaching drama, as a way of having focus in improvisation for the theatre. Since then they have become essential questions for us in our creative work.

Who is this Book For?

This book is for all people who work and play with children – parents and foster parents, play workers and play therapists, nursery nurses and teachers, psychologists and child therapists, paediatricians, and Child Protection teams. The list of people who hold the welfare of children as paramount seems endless; yet the sheer volume of children who are at risk is at times overwhelming. I hope that this book can assist all of these people to tell stories and play in ways which are fulfilling and helpful to the children in their care.

What Can this Book Do?

This book is not a therapy book as such, but its methods and techniques can be incorporated into any child therapist's way of working. People are working with children in many ways – nurture groups, playgroups, recreational groups, 'time out', counselling, play therapy, assessment, hospital play, and community play – the majority of which involve the healing properties of play itself, without it being 'therapy' specifically.

Why this Book?

I was moved to write this book out of my own work with children in therapy and school, as well as being a mother and a grandmother. Although there is a greater awareness of the importance of stories and play for children, it still is not central to our way of thinking about the world and how children thrive. For example, discipline is often cited as being important; yet what better way to learn discipline and concern for others, than through the medium of play? What can give us structure and security in our lives but the story, with a beginning, middle and an ending?

When is this Book Useful?

The ideas in this book can be used as part of a syllabus on training courses and as a refresher for our practice. The practical material can be integrated into your existing practices when working with children, together with the underlying theory that explains the suggested methods. There are examples that can be applied to groups as well as to individual children, and in one-off sessions as well as in continuing programmes. The book is designed so that activities are presented in context, with the ideas behind the work examined and described. However, if you are feeling drained and exhausted, this book might help you to find some inspiration, although I would suggest checking your stress levels too! Maybe find a story that is just for you.

Where is this Book Appropriate?

This book can be a resource in many different settings – the school, the home, the clinic, and the play-group. It is important that we are able to see story telling and playing as infinitely adaptable and creative, as ways of enriching our work and our lives. However, it is equally important to create a special time and place for our stories. The story room and the play room that have a space for stories help to create the boundaries of our work, and enable children to focus on the immediate matter in hand. It may be that a toy or puppet is needed to assist in the story telling, or the listening, or the asking of a question.

How are the Activities Applied?

The ideas and techniques in this book can be applied as part of your continuing play work or play therapy, or you may decide to create a story time with an individual or group that you feel is 'at risk'. Stories can be integrated into all forms of play, as well as the education and nurture of children with special needs.

The answers to the questions above have mainly been about the 'mechanics' of storytelling: who will do it, where, and so on. Let us now ask the same questions again – what I would call the real questions – in relation to the child.

Who are the Activities For?

Children come to see us because they have stories to tell. They may be stories of trauma and abuse, or they may be stories about not being heard. They may also be stories that are 'never to be told', as the magpie song tells us. 'Children at risk' is a term that belongs to the past, the present and the future. The child may have been abused, and never told their story; they may currently be having nightmares, and need help to deal with them; or they may be at risk of developmental delay, and need some intervention in order to maximise their potential.

What Will They Do?

Children are infinitely creative with their stories and their play, and can find many ways through their difficulties with our prompting and support. If children feel secure, protected, and respected when it is story time, they will share their stories with us. They need to know that they have our attention.

> Scene on a bus: A boy of about seven is trying to get his mother's attention, but she is heavily engrossed in gossip with her friend. The boy keeps tugging at her sleeve, saying 'Mum, Mum', but is completely ignored. The boy then says, 'Why did the chicken cross the road?' His mother, without looking at him, and scarcely pausing in her conversation, says 'To get to the other side.' The boy replies, 'No, you are wrong: he crossed the road to look for some food – and then he got run over – he was all squashed in the road – and all the blood ran out – he was really squashed – aren't I right?' 'Yes, now be quiet', says Mum, without looking round or interrupting her conversation. Nothing that the boy said to her has been 'heard'.

Children may tell their stories through the variety of materials that we have in our story room, and it is important that we have plenty of choice. Children may make requests for very specific media – for example, glitter glue pens, stickers, sludge, and goo. It is important to see these requests as the child finding ways of communicating with us.

Why is this Important?

Stories and play have been essential parts of our lives since our ancient past, and across many cultures. The break-up of societies, communities, and families can cause a disruption to our roots and leave us disorientated and confused. Part of our work lies in replacing gaps in children's experience, in order for them to re-connect with their roots. The other part is for children to find stories, through action and symbols, in order to express muddled and confused experiences and feelings. Stories can help a child find the way again.

We need to remember that, for most of the children that we work with, there is no choice of road: their life's journey has already been mapped out, and the outcome will be inevitable unless we can intervene in some way. Stories can help children find that second road, and to understand that, somewhere along the line, there can be a change of direction. It is possible to find a new signpost.

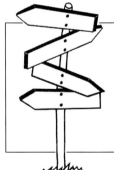

This way, that way, where shall I go?
The signpost has gone and I am far from home.
Should I go up, or should I go down?
Make a wish and jump, and then I will know.

When Does a Child Need Stories?

Children always need stories! Probably the first time that a child gets the sense of a story is when mothers tell stories and plans to their unborn children. Pregnant women with time alone will often engage in creative communication with the yet-to-be-born infant (Jennings, 1999), and sing, tell stories, or have an imaginary conversation. Stories have the structure to create security (the beginning, middle, and end), and therefore have a calming effect on turbulent children. They can be told at any time, but perhaps need to take place at a time that is specially dedicated to storytelling – bedtime, of course, the end of a play session, or as focus of the play therapy session. If you are seeing a child or group over a period of time, the story can be told in instalments, or a favourite can be repeated, sometimes over and over again. It is important to remember that a child derives far more from the human element of a person telling a story than by hearing it on tapes and television. Story tapes are supplementary stories, and, as we know, are invaluable on long car journeys.

Where Will The Stories be Told?

Generally, wherever there is a gathering of children who want to listen there can be a story.

Stories can be told indoors or outdoors, upstairs or downstairs. However, it is preferable to have a quiet space – the story corner in the play room or the playground, or the quiet space in the play therapy room are ideal. It is important for children to be able to differentiate space and designate it for different activities and experiences – the opposite, in fact, of the person walking down the road, speaking on a mobile phone, and eating a sandwich! The story space can have pictures on the walls depicting different stories, and pictures or toys to provide characters for the tale. Sand-tray characters and objects can be made use of in the storytelling process, both for the adult as well as the child. Perhaps you can divide up the space for quiet story telling, action work, and messy work. This is ideal if you have a big enough space, but many people have to share a room and bring equipment in and out, and the space available can be very small. However, we can bring in containers of toys and art materials, and have one picture or object, such as the magic story stone, that creates the space for story work.

How Will the Child Tell Stories?

Children tell stories through whatever media they have to hand. Initially, they may be fearful and anxious, and not want to speak at all; they may wait to be prompted or to make sure they 'do it right'. They may be so exuberant that the session is all action and very little story! However, if we observe children at play, they usually tell stories through actions that they have made up or that they have heard or seen. Children enact stories, and we can learn much from observing them unobtrusively.

If the stories are part of therapeutic play, it is important for you and the child (as well as the referring organisation or family) to agree on what the sessions are for, and what they are about. What happens to the stories that the child tells? How do you agree a 'contract', in terms of being explicit about what your sessions are about? If there are worrying features in the story, you need to discuss them with your supervisor in case intervention is needed, such as a child being removed to a place of safety; but unless this is your brief, the story telling is not specifically for disclosure work. Nevertheless, if disclosure takes place, you need to be able to contain it within the story work, and take advice on the next step. Your agreement needs to include an understanding that you may share material with your supervisor or referral team if there are concerns for the safety of the child or the safety of others. Most authorities and professional bodies have standard agreements, and a template is provided at the end of this chapter.

Let us now ask the six questions about you, the play and story worker, to help you make decisions about the application of these ideas in your work.

Who Are You?

And I don't mean your age and qualifications in this context! Who are you in relation to storytelling? Do you enjoy storytelling, or listening to stories? Are you comfortable in the role of storyteller, or do you feel you do not know enough stories? It is fine to read stories out loud: indeed, many children expect this from us.

At the end of every chapter are some ideas and worksheets for you to try and to encourage you to feel able to develop your own ideas. Maybe it feels difficult to make up stories that are appropriate for the child. That is fine – it takes practice, if you are not familiar with storytelling yourself; but I can assure you that it is easier than you think. Maybe you have memories of standing up in class at school and having to read out something that you had written; perhaps you are anxious because it may not be 'right', and others may laugh at you. Maybe you loved making up stories when you were younger, but your teacher did not encourage creativity, and you had remarks on your school report such as, 'Mary lets her imagination run away with her: she needs to learn to concentrate.' Whatever your past experiences that have been unhelpful, make a decision to leave them behind and to start as a storyteller right now. Pick up three different things that are in the room, place them in front of you, and start to make up a story involving the objects. There are some story sheets at the end of this chapter to give both you and the children ideas.

What Will You Do?

First of all find a quiet space for yourself where you can write down and think about a favourite story from your childhood. The more you can understand the impact a story has made on you, the more you will understand about yourself and storytelling. It then follows that you will understand the impact of stories on children, and that certain stories, both personal and fictional, can stay with them for life – just as yours have stayed with you. Find opportunities to tell stories to other people – for example, your own children or grandchildren, your neighbour's or friend's children. You could start a small storytelling group in a school holiday to develop your stories.

A wonderful resource for new stories is the internet, where we can find stories from many different countries around the world. Nevertheless, this does not rule out all the traditional stories we have learned, and local stories that older members of our family can perhaps recall for us. What stories are passed down the family about relatives who ran away to sea, disappeared, or did something that 'we don't talk about'? Build up a picture of your own family through the stories you gather, and note how different family members will have a different version of the story. It is useful to ask them, 'Do you remember when...? What really happened?' There will be myriad responses because individuals tell the stories from their own point of view. This is an important point to remember when working with children: we need to be able to tell stories from their point of view, as well as our own, especially when we are offering them a story as a gift when they are troubled, as described in Chapter 8.

What Happened?

Why Are You Telling Stories?

Maybe you have been storytelling for a long time, and it is difficult to remember when you first started; or perhaps you just slid into it as something you enjoyed doing. However, it may be that this is a new beginning, and you are not quite sure 'why?' You have thought about the 'Who?' and the 'What?' Is there a 'why?' 'Why?' questions are always more difficult than others because they can include some very parental messages – 'Why do you want to stay out?' or 'Why do you want to stop/ join/buy/take various activities?'– and there is often a sense of disapproval, leading us to justify what we are doing. Consider the following 'Why?' responses to different situations.

Teenager is creeping quietly into the house after school because he knows that mother is unwell, and he does not want to disturb her. Mother calls out, 'Why are you moving around so secretly? What are you up to?'

Child is desperately trying to cut out and glue a picture for her granny's birthday. Parent comes in and says, 'Why do you always have to make such a mess?'

Child comes in and says to parent, 'Can I go round and visit Jane's house?' Parent replies, 'Why do you want to go there?'

Write in your story book any situations from the past when you were asked 'Why?' and felt uncomfortable or put on the spot.

When Will You Tell Stories?

Storytelling with children at risk takes time, and it is important that we do not just tack it on to something else we are doing. We need time for preparation, time to gather stories, and time to be clear about why we are working with one particular story rather than another. If a session turns out unexpectedly, can we be flexible and change our plans?

In the resource chapter at the end of this book you will find information about many books on storytelling. Books by Alida Gersie are especially important to assist us with our storytelling: she is an expert in this field, and has created her concept of 'Storymaking' which can be learned and applied with many different groups of people, as well as individual children and adults.

Where Will You Tell Stories?

We have talked earlier about the space we may use for storytelling, and have suggested that it needs to be a quiet space, whether indoors or outdoors. If you are trying out informal storytelling, it can be round the kitchen table with a drink and biscuits, in the garden under a tree, or in the sitting room – with the television off, and no interruptions from mobile phones! We talk about 'sensory bombardment' in Chapter 6, and it is important that we make sure we can slow down the pace and create a safe place in which to begin the storytelling with phrases like, 'Once upon a Time …' or 'Over the hills and far away …' or 'And so it was …' What we are now describing is not just the space but the fact that it needs to be conducive to storytelling. Perhaps we are beginning to get ideas for our 'storytelling role', which maybe a little different from our other roles.

How Shall I Tell Stories?

My immediate response to this question is 'with an open heart and an open mind'. The most important thing for children is that they can sense our honesty and the fact that we are authentic, that we believe in what we are doing. We can enhance our storytelling role by developing our voices, and by being mindful of our rhythm of storytelling, creating pauses and a sense of occasion. These skills develop over time. When I speak of the development of the voice, I am sure that we can all recall voices that we did not listen to: they were on a flat monotone, were too shrill, or they were inaudible or too loud. Listening to our own voice, and developing its range and depth, will enhance our storytelling in very creative ways.

We may create our ground rules and our structures, our permissions and our plans, but let us put the creativity of stories at the centre of what we do. We tell stories because it is something we love doing and would like to share with others. We listen to stories because we know it is an important means for a child to express him or herself, especially in times of trouble or trauma. It is now time to put all of these considerations into practice.

Telling My Own Story

How long is it since you thought about stories that you have enjoyed in your life, both as a child and as an adult? As a child, can you recall being read to, or did you mainly read stories yourself? Can you recall a specific story that you enjoyed hearing or reading over and over again? Write a summary of the story in your story-book, and try to recall the time and place it was told. You may like to illustrate it with a picture as well, and to recall the feelings that accompanied the story, even when you knew the story 'inside out'. You will return to it later on in this Chapter.

My vivid memory is of a book called *The Black Riders* by Violet Needham, which recounts the adventures of an 11-year-old orphan boy, who was fostered by a kind rural couple. He learns all about natural lore, and leads a lonely but contented life in the forest and countryside, watching people go along the main highway. Unwittingly he is drawn into an underground movement, led by Far Away Moses. Eventually the boy and Moses are captured, and the boy has to face Count Jasper the Terrible. He is the only person who can look the Count in the eye and say 'No' to him. In the end, after a lot of hair-raising situations, there is an amnesty, and the regime of Jasper the Terrible becomes more moderate.

Processing this story as an adult, I can see several strands that had a very profound meaning for me, and continued to do so throughout my adult life. However, I was not aware of this until I had a dream as an adult, in which I woke up saying a line from the book! The story of *The Black Riders* contains the following contrasts:

- Freedom of ideas, and oppressive dictatorship.
- Rural life-style, and city life-style.
- 'Rough hands' of the foster mother and 'perfumed silk' of the lady in the big house.
- The endless road, and the confines of the walled city.
- Discussion and negotiation, and the imposition of will.
- Self-regulation, and imposed regime.
- The choice between two roads.
- Far Away Moses and Jasper the Terrible.

All of these themes are relevant to my life-style as well as to the way that I work with children, including my own. In many ways there is a lot of adult political thinking in the book, which, as a ten-year-old, I was able to understand and ponder. The important thing is that it contains paradoxes and a negotiated resolution, rather than a 'quick fix', 'happy ever after', and 'nothing changes' style of ending. Think about the story that you have recalled, and look at the several themes that are followed through. How do they relate to your own development and issues? Have you found a compromise? Write some more reflections in your story-book about the importance of stories in your life. What are the dominant themes and contrasts? How can the stories that you already know be helpful to the children in your care? Think about the choice between two roads. If you can, find and read the poem by Robert Frost called 'The Road Not Taken' which ends with the following lines:

> Two roads diverged in a wood, and I –
> I took the one less traveled by,
> And that has made all the difference.

Ask yourself if you have ever had to make that choice, or whether you wish you had taken the other road. Maybe there are some compromises for you to make in your own life now.

Worksheet 5
Which Way Am I Going?

Name _____   Date _____

When I look at my signpost I want to choose

_____

_____

_____

_____

_____

_____

_____

Agreement for Story Sharing and Play

This agreement is made between

Child's name _____

and

Therapist's name _____

We will meet on a regular basis at _____ *(place)*

from _____ to _____ *(time)*

for _____ *(number)* sessions for playing and telling stories.

This is a private time for me to talk about myself through play and stories, especially things that are troubling me or make me fearful.

I understand that someone else may be told if I need additional help, or if I am not safe. My stories and pictures stay in the story room until all the sessions are completed, and then I can choose what happens to them. If they are to be shared with other professional people, I will be asked first.

Signed *(child)* _____

Signed *(worker)* _____

Signed *(family/authority if appropriate)* _____

_____

Story Sheet 1

Name _____ Date _____

The story of _____

_____

_____

_____

_____

_____

_____

_____

_____

Story Sheet 2

Name _____ Date _____

The story of _____

_____

_____

_____

_____

_____

_____

_____

Story Sheet 3

Name _____ Date _____

The story of _____

_____

_____

_____

_____

_____

_____

_____

Story Sheet 4

Name _____ Date _____

The story of _____

_____

_____

_____

_____

_____

_____

_____

_____

P This page may be photocopied for instructional use only. *Creative Storytelling* © Sue Jennings 2004

Story Sheet S

Name _____ Date _____

The story of _____

_____

_____

_____

_____

_____

_____

_____

CHAPTER 4

Children's Stories and Play Development

Introduction

THIS CHAPTER IS ABOUT how play develops in children up to seven years of age, and the three stages of Embodiment – Project – Role. These stages are important because they allow various aspects of the child's attachment, behaviour and personality to develop. We look at the possible strategies in play that compensate for stages that have been missed.

Many theories of child development do not include references to storytelling and play. Theorists usually focus either on an orientation towards a psychological theory, and reflect the theorist's own stance; or they are concerned with observation, such as physical or cognitive skill, and create a system from their observations. The orientation theorists require that we accept the given basis for the theory, while the observational theorists provide us with data that relates tasks to age stages – data that we can readily observe in our work. Some theorists from both groups include play in their observations, but no one until Slade (1954) and Courtney and Schattner (1982) gave a central focus to play development.

Slade and Courtney are two of the early writers who provide us with developmental stages of dramatic play, and both see that these stages are essential for life itself, as well as for precursers for further creative developments through the arts. Previously, play had been included as part of overall child development. We shall now look at a developmental paradigm that can form the basis of both play and play therapy, within any theoretical framework and application, and which leads into assessment of play and storytelling.

The main underlying theory of this book is Embodiment – Projection – Role (EPR), through which we can structure the most appropriate intervention for a child's dramatic play and active storytelling. This is especially important when the child is at risk, and may have missed out on the crucial milestones in early learning. EPR is the basis of the Playtherapy Method, (Jennings, 1999). It is a developmental paradigm that charts the progression of a child's dramatic play from birth to seven years of age. Based on extended observation of babies, young children and pregnant women, it provides a parallel progression alongside other developmental processes, such as physical, cognitive, emotional and social development.

EPR is 'value free': it does not rely on a particular school of psychological theory, and, indeed, can be integrated into any psychological model, or therapeutic or educational practice. EPR charts 'dramatic development', which is the basis of the child being able to enter the world of imagination and symbol, the world of dramatic play and drama. The early attachment between mother and infant has a strong dramatic component, through playfulness and role-reversal, which is an extension of the dramatic relationship the mother forms with her unborn child.

Embodiment

During the Embodiment stage the child's early experiences are physical, and are expressed mainly through bodily movement and the senses. The child is learning through the way he or she is held or not held, and whether the senses are being stimulated or satisfied. These physical experiences are essential for the development of the 'body-self': we cannot have a body image until we have a body-self, and the child needs to be able to 'live' in his or her body. The child is also learning about different body parts and their coordination, and developing confidence to move in space. Many singing games and nursery rhymes are about the senses and the different parts of the body, and involve hearing, seeing, tasting, touching, smelling, or the naming of different body parts. For example, 'The Cow Goes Moo' is about different sounds; 'Incy-wincy Spider' is very visual; 'Pat-a-cake Baker's Man' anticipates food; 'The Rain Maker' is about touch and sound; 'The Flower Fairy' is about sweet smells; and 'Two Eyes Peeping' names hands, thumbs, fingers, toes, head, eyes and nose.

Many children have been deprived of their sensory experience, through neglect or bombardment of the senses, and much of our storytelling may have to involve very simple sensory exercises. For example, you can have a Sense Box (see Chapter 6: Stories and Games for Our Senses) filled with a wide range of textured objects, such as velvet, sandpaper, satin, bristles, and plasticine. The game involves closing our eyes or looking away, and trying to recognise the different textures, giving words to describe them. The child may know the materials, or may start to find words to describe them: 'This is very scratchy, and this is smooth'. From this beginning, a simple story can emerge: 'The scratchy dog made friends with the smooth cat, and they decided to go for a walk; and then …'. If you ask a child what a texture feels like, it is the beginning not only of an exploration of the senses, but also of feelings.

We know that children at risk often have great difficulty in expressing their feelings, and, if they have been abused, they may have shut themselves off from their feelings completely. Working through the Embodiment stage with the senses can be a slow re-connection, not only to sensing, but also to feeling.

A Sense Box can also include materials to explore all the senses such as: a small bell, a wrapped sweet, a hologram, a perfume sample and a soft toy. Sense Boxes can also be created for each of the senses, or the child can create a personal Sense Box, perhaps with your assistance. Not all sensory exercises are based on action: you will also have, if possible, a rest corner, where there are blankets, a feeding bottle, and cuddly toys, and where soothing stories (such as *I love you Blue Kangaroo* or *Willy and Hugh*) can be read.

The Embodiment stage can involve stories and dramatic play in the different modes of expression, and can include the following:

- Gross body movement (involving the whole body).
- Fine body movement (involving different parts of the body).
- Sensory movement (involving textures, sound, taste, smell and sight).
- Singing games that involve naming body parts as they are touched.
- Rhythmic movement and dance.
- Sword play and wrestling.
- Creative ideas for movement (for example, moving as a monster, alien, or mouse).
- Stories with sounds and movements.

We shall explore these modes further in Chapter 6, together with more examples of stories and techniques. However, it is important to note down any of your own reactions to what you have read so far. It may be that these include discomfort at the idea of physical work or body contact. Some organisations do not allow touch, either through fear of litigation or because they prefer to emphasise projective and verbal, rather than sensory and physical, play. If you choose to work in a way that involves body contact, parents and children need to understand that play therapy may involve touch, and must agree to it in your contract. Agreed touch can be very healing within the play: it still leaves the child in control, and is not imposed by the therapist or leader.

Transition One

The change-over from the Embodiment stage to the Projective stage, which usually takes place at around 12-14 months of age, is a time of transition, and has a 'marker' such as a soft toy, blanket, or piece of material. This 'marker' or 'object' is described by Winnicott (1974) as the 'transitional object'. Both texture and smell are important, so the marker is linked to the child's sensory experience. It is usually considered to be the child's first symbol, representing the absent mother. The transitional object is both ritualised and creative: it has to stay the same, even though it might become grubby; and it is given a name, but it also changes – for example, it can become a 'mask' to hide behind, a blanket for a doll, or a scarf for a costume. It integrates the paradox of being the same and being different, through the way it is played with, talked to, and cuddled. Children who come to play or for play therapy often need this relationship with a cuddly item as part of their re-development, and you can make up songs and stories about the teddy or the blanket with the child.

Teddy Story

Once upon a time, a teddy called … was lost in the meadow, and it started to rain so she got very very wet. A child called … was going for a walk, and found the wet teddy and decided to take her home. … put her under his or her raincoat to keep her dry, and the child's sweater got soaking wet. When … got home, the teddy and the sweater had to be dried, but then they could have a big warm and dry cuddle.

Projection

During the Projection stage the child is responding to the world beyond the body, to things outside the body. The child's responses may well be physical – for example, when a child plays with finger paint, the important point is that the paint is a substance outside the body boundaries. As the Projection stage develops, children not only relate to different objects and substances, but also place them together in shapes and constellations. We see an increasing use of stories with objects such as the doll's house or puppets. The play in this stage is either exploratory, or repetitious and ritualised. Just as with Embodiment, it integrates the known and the unknown. Children who have been deprived of play experiences can be quite overwhelmed by the plethora of objects and stimuli in the play room, and may spend time exploring a lot of things. The child may request certain things to be there, but usually there are enough choices to allow the child to play in the way he or she chooses.

In the early stages of Projective play, some children may feel anxious about making a permanent creation, such as a drawing or model, especially if they have been subject to sarcasm or ridicule. They may feel that it has to be a 'good picture', or that there is a certain picture that you want them to make. For some children, a blank piece of paper can be very daunting, so colouring in a picture can be reassuring. The picture can then be used to create a story. The different modes of Projection in this developmental stage include:

- Play with substance (sand, water, finger paint, clay, Plasticine).
- Play with pictures (crayons, paints, drawing, collage with varied media).
- Play with bricks, puzzles and counters (patterns, constructions, 'all fall down').
- Play with toys (sand-tray stories, sculpts).
- Play with scenes (doll's house, puppets and the making of puppets).
- Play with natural media (pebbles, bark, twigs, leaves).

Transition Two

The second stage of transition emerges as the child is less involved in projecting stories and scenes through the puppets and toys, and begins briefly to take on the roles and characters. This is a form of pre-dramatic play where there is a particular prop or costume that is important. This second transition may be marked with a different kind of object, which may be an object of authority – for example, a stick or a sword, or a specific costume that allows the child to take control, directing the action as well as being a part of it. Harry Potter's magic wand is a prime example of this, and a simple stick that had fallen off the branch of a tree served as the wand for one of my young clients. He was devastated when the piece of stick broke, and the play could not continue until we improvised a similar wand.

Towards the end of the Projection stage, the child's play becomes increasingly dramatised, with stories and scenes being enacted from newly created stories, or stories that already exist. Children at this stage are developing their own narrative structure (stories that have a beginning, a middle and an end) and are increasing their capacity for 'free play' – what adults would term 'improvisation', where you start with a topic or an object and see where it goes. We could also refer to free play as 'stream of consciousness', which may well feed into a later narrative structure, and is a quality that is invaluable as a life skill. During this transition we can observe children become their own directors and the directors of others, as they organise 'events' and create plays in which they both perform and direct. They are able to exist separately with their creativity, as well as being part of a pair or small group.

Role

The Role stage is characterised by the child's capacity to take on and sustain a role within a story or piece of dramatic play. They will often take on more than one role in a story, and involve us in the cast as well. The scenes may be from well-known stories or children's own versions of them, as well as television tales and dramas. The children may well be re-creating episodes from their own lives, through metaphoric stories that enable us to witness, and they to communicate, the reality of what they are having to live.

The Role stage is very complex in all children because it involves them making sense of something in their own lives. It also involves many other sorts of stories, and there is a growing sense of artistic and joyous awareness: the child is beginning to be aware of his or her own powers of creativity. There is a development of 'what is right' for a scene or a role – 'Mummies don't do that', or 'Monsters walk like this'. Not only are roles acted, but scenes are directed, and there is an increasing awareness of design. This can be a very healing process for damaged children, as they begin to create for themselves, and have a witness to the creation. We need to be careful not only to understand the child's distress, but also to understand how the child is directing his or her own recovery.

There are many ways of creating dramatised stories through the Role stage:

- Use simple roles with single feelings (the angry person, the sad person).
- Create animal characters that interact.

- Use favourite stories to enact together.
- Use the dressing-up box, and allow a dramatised story to emerge.
- Use a mask as a starting point for a story.
- Use the idea of writing a television script together, and then enact it.
- Use ideas that have been generated through projective play.

'Let's Make a Play'

The following short script gives an example of the sort of dramatised story that is useful at this stage.

The Queen and the Vampire

(Enter the Queen.)

QUEEN: Hello everyone: I'm the Queen, and I'm trying to escape from a nasty vampire who is on the prowl.

VAMPIRE: I'm the vampire, and I'm on the look-out for pretty young queens such as she.

(Queen goes to side of stage to consult her mother.)

QUEEN: Mother, I am really worried about this nasty vampire who is chasing after pretty young queens. What shall I do? How can I get rid of him?

MOTHER: Stop Worrying! You've just got to stand up for yourself. Tell you what, get a sword and poke it at the Vampire, then throw him into jail if he doesn't behave himself.

(Queen returns to centre stage, with a sword she has found. Vampire reappears.)

QUEEN: Now then, don't you think you can be nasty to me! *(Queen pokes sword at Vampire's mask.)* Drop your mask!

(Queen hits Vampire's mask – on floor – fiercely.)

VAMPIRE: *(Whimpering.)* I can't be a proper Vampire any more now my mask is off. I don't know what to do!

(Queen impatiently shoves Vampire into jail.)

QUEEN: You can jolly well stay in there!

VAMPIRE: I'm hungry. If I can't be a proper Vampire, let me out of jail so I can come for my tea and have my beans on toast!

QUEEN: No: you will have to stay in there and die!

VAMPIRE: Please let me out. I'll grant you three wishes if you let me out of here. Please, Your Majesty!

QUEEN: All right, give me three wishes.

VAMPIRE: What wishes do you want to make Your Majesty?

QUEEN: First, I want you to be good! Second, I want to be the most popular Queen. Third, I want to be wise, and know everything I need to know!

(Vampire waves his magic wand, uttering a spell.)

VAMPIRE: Abracadabra, Allacazoo, I'm going to make your wishes come true! Now all your wishes will come true. *(Queen lets Vampire out of jail.)* Oh Good, I'm free, free at last!

QUEEN: Just a minute! How do I know you're going to be good? You will have to go back in jail if I catch you up to your old tricks again!

VAMPIRE: I'll try – but s'pose I make a mistake. How shall I know what being good really means? You are the most popular Queen: you are wise. You must guide me. Tell me what I must do to be good.

(Queen agrees to write down rules for being good so the Vampire doesn't forget.)

QUEEN: *(Reading her proclamation.)*
               The Rules are:

1 Be nice to my Mum and Dad
2 Say 'Please' and 'Thank You' to people
3 Say 'Sorry' when you make a mistake.

VAMPIRE: Thank you so much, Your Majesty. I promise I'll try really hard to be good.

QUEEN: I'm very pleased to hear that.

As children's storytelling and dramatic play develop we can observe that they have integrated all three stages: Embodiment, Projection and Role (EPR). They create plays with movement, costumes and props, and various characters. Usually the three stages of EPR are completed by the age of seven years. However, things do not stop there: we continue to visit these stages in pre-teen and teenage development, although not always in the EPR sequence. Embodiment, Projection and Role are experimented with, tried and tested as identity continues to develop. Finally we make choices as adults based on the stage that we have dominance in, and usually take up jobs and hobbies that have either an Embodiment, Projection or Role focus (Jennings, 1998).

Mead should have said that we … actually feel some pain by this pretending pain. By yelling as if you were scared you get scared. By weeping you get sad. By dancing with a person you fall in love. By taking the part of a role play you can become the person you are acting. The play of children is full of this wonderful self-generating expressivity. (Berg, 1998)

Competence in EPR is essential for a child's maturation:

- It creates the core of attachment between mother and infant.
- It forms a basis for the growth of identity and independence.
- It establishes the 'dramatised body' – the body that can create.
- It strengthens and further develops the imagination.
- It contributes to a child's resilience through 'ritual and risk'.
- It enables a child to move from 'everyday reality' to 'dramatic reality' and back again, appropriately.
- It facilitates problem solving and conflict resolution.
- It provides role play and dramatic play, which in turn create flexibility.
- It gives a child the experience and skills to be part of the social world.

Embodiment – Projection – Role are stages of all human development: children and adults are impoverished or unwell if these stages have not been successfully navigated. Application of EPR with children at risk or with special needs provides an opportunity for a child's re-development, as well as providing a structure for appropriate play and playtherapy.

> Anything is possible within the drama, and the dramatic play gives permission to do things that in everyday life would not be permissible or wholesome. (Jennings, 2002)

Further Observations on EPR in Practice

In a dramatic play it is important for children to play 'distanced' roles, ie, roles that are not in their immediate life experience. The Jester play is a good example of a child playing out and understanding her life issues through a distanced play. This would not be possible if the drama was too close to her own experience. 'This is the paradox of drama: that I come closer by being more distanced.' (Jennings, 1998)

One of the hardest things for the therapist to handle is not giving the child explanations and interpretations. We do not like 'not knowing': we want to know what is going on, and have invented interpretation in order to explain things and probably reduce our own anxiety. At another level we 'know' what is going on, and certainly the child knows. Maybe we have to learn to bear 'not knowing'; to stay with the chaos, and allow the meaning to emerge.

Horley (1998) has done extensive research using the EPR method in order to identify children who are 'non-players'. She suggests that dramatic play is a 'situation where role playing becomes more complex and includes dressing up, developing dialogue and creating environments within which to play different roles. Scenes and stories are enacted with peers being included, although there may be some situations of a child playing in a dramatic way on their own'.

EPR can be integrated into all approaches of psychology and play therapy, although it works more efficiently where therapist and child can create the scenes and activities together. The early roots of EPR can be traced to pre-birth experience in the dramatised relationship between mother and unborn child (Jennings, 1998, 1999), so we can say that the infant is born already 'dramatised'. It is important that therapists using EPR re-experience the stages for themselves, as well as making observations of children in these stages. This research is still being developed, and play therapists are encouraged to test it in their own research.

Movement

Most of our early physical and bodily experience comes through our proximity to others, usually our mothers or carers. (In this book I shall continue to use the word 'mother' in the generic sense of the person who cares for us.) We are cradled and rocked as we co-operate with rhythmic rocking and singing. Babies and mothers co-respond within the collaborative approach of physical expression. Already the movement has 'ritualised and risk' qualities: on the one hand we have repetitive rocking movements, on the other, we bounce up and down with glee. However, many children have had early physical experiences that are not always positive, and they may need to take very small steps as their physical experiences become safe again. For example, soothing movement may have been used for grooming a child, which can later lead into sexual abuse, or sudden movement may have been part of a violent reaction from an adult towards a child.

Physical play is a crucial stage of development for infants because the body is the primary means of learning (Jennings, 1990), and all other learning is secondary to that first learned through the body. Children with bodily trauma therefore need extended physical play in order to re-build a healthy and confident body. A child's embodiment development can be distorted through the following:

- Being 'over-held': the child who is over-protected, and over-dependent. There is a perpetual fused state, and a blurring of body boundaries. The child is always physically with the mother, and has never been separated and played 'against' her, (Sherborne, 1990, 2001). The child has never developed an experience of who is 'me' and who is 'not me'.
- Being 'under-held': the child who is left for long periods of time in isolation. A child in this situation develops anxiety rather than autonomy, is mistrustful, and often confused about body and spatial boundaries. The child may become flat and withdrawn, and eventually fail to thrive.
- Being violated through physical or sexual abuse. The child's bodily boundaries are invaded, resulting in trauma and confusion: there is often fear and anxiety, and an avoidance of physical contact. The child may express extreme physical rage, or inappropriate touch.

As we noted earlier, many teachers, workers and therapists, find it difficult to consider using Embodiment in their work because of traumatic experiences in the child's or adult's past, or because of the ever-present fear of misunderstood touch and possible litigation. There are several movement solutions for the facilitator who is reluctant to touch: not all movement has to involve contact, and there are many healing movement games for the child and worker to do together. You may also work with various 'props', such as hoops, string, or silk scarves. In this way a contact with the child is established through the scarf – this is especially useful when working with autistic children. You can also work with groups and do group movement, which is very good for social development – first work in pairs, then threes, and so on. Make sure you include collaborative movement, such as balancing and trust walks, as well as assertive movement, such as pushing and pulling exercises (Sherborne, 2001).

Movement games and exercises can all lead into more extended storytelling, and all stories can be told through movement. The stories can be helped by having a supply of material pieces to assist the movement and create the characters. Fabric can be used for wings or capes, or to create a wind or ripply movement. You will find that the child's physical involvement in the embodied story will, in itself, bring about change. However, you need to be involved as well!

The world of stories is so vast that you may be thinking, 'Where do I start?' In your notebook, write down headings for all the stories you can recall in five minutes. The list is bound to include some fairy stories, folk stories, and perhaps vague remembrances of children's classics.

Our lists usually include the story of Cinderella, and it is a story we are tempted to use because it is the rags to riches story of an abused little girl. The difficulty with the story in relation to our work is that it completely misses out Cinderella's development as a strong, independent young woman. Cinderella goes from one kindly rescuer to a passionate prince, with little room for her own individuality and choices. This is where we need to develop skills of improvisation, and find ways of building choices into well-known story structures. Having said that, 'Cinderella' lends itself very well to a physical re-enactment with some of the following ideas:

- Thin people and fat people.
- A fairy godmother with a magic wand.
- Mice and ponies, and royalty dancing in a palace.
- Weak fathers and cruel sisters.
- Difficulties of step-families.
- Benign and magical helpers: Buttons and the Fairy Godmother.
- Cinderella being seen in her own right.
- Variation in the ending to build up strengths and resilience.

Worksheets 6 and 7 are an example of how you can explore Cinderella with an individual child or group. You can create the rules for the safe place in a Proclamation or decide where to ride in your Golden Coach.

Telling My Own Story

Think about your own development through Embodiment – Projection – Role. Do you feel more at home with physical activities such as dancing or sport? Or do you like writing, drawing, or cooking? Maybe you prefer to take on different roles such as sitting on committees and fundraising, or trade union stewarding? What about when you were young? Write down the different ways that you played, and what you really enjoyed before the age of eight years. Has there been a similar pattern throughout your life, or have things changed as you have grown up? For example, if you played a lot with drawing and bricks as a child, do you feel most at home in projective activities now? In your work? In your social and private life?

I remember vividly creating my own dances and plays, as well as clubs and charters which I wanted other children to join! I went to a village school with two rooms – the big room and the little room (the adjectives refer to the age of the children, not the size of the room!). There was a lot of teasing, especially boys pulling the girls' plaits so, at nine years of age, I formed the 'Leave the Boys Alone Club' – LBAC. Five of us girls had meetings and formed our rules, but two girls left quickly because it was more fun to tease the boys. It seemed an early example of me trying to find alternative strategies to bullying rather than telling tales or fighting back. Do you find any mirror between how you were as a child and what you do now?

Name _____ Date _____

PROCLAMATION

I want to create the following new rules in the life of this kingdom:

_____

_____

_____

_____

_____

_____

_____

Worksheet 7
My Golden Coach

Name _____ Date _____

In my golden coach I will travel to

_____
_____
_____
_____

I will leave behind

_____
_____
_____
_____
_____
_____
_____
_____

CHAPTER 5

Stories and Pictures for Assessment

Introduction

FOR MANY PEOPLE THE very word 'assessment' can conjure up ideas of judgement, and power, or of somehow finding people lacking or unworthy. Yet, responsibly and creatively applied, assessment can make sure that children receive relevant help, and that the most appropriate form of story work and play therapy is available to them. In this Chapter we will consider various forms of assessment that we can use in our story work, and use stories themselves as part of an assessment procedure.

What Do We Sense About the Child?

When we first receive the referral letter or telephone call, what is our first gut reaction? Do we have any hunches? Does the description of the child remind us of a fairy story? These first intuitions are important, and we need to log them before moving on to more formal assessment. What feelings are conjured up in ourselves? Are these feelings connected with our own childhood, or will our own feelings help us to understand the child?

What do we see when we first meet the child? Are our hunches confirmed, or are we seeing someone very different from who we imagined? We may observe that the child is physically malnourished, or that their eyes are glazed; he or she may be fidgeting, pacing, restless, rocking. They may be absolutely still and seem to be cut off, or they may be flooding with tears, self-harming, muttering threats, or hearing voices that we are unable to hear. As we stay with someone 'in the moment', we are observing and noting with all our senses. We are aware of what we feel we can assist with, within our own frame of expertise, and what needs further specialist help – for example from a family doctor, the child's family, social services, or child support agencies. It is important to make use of any networks that we know the child already has, or that could be helpful to them or the family. We may feel we need some advice, and time for reflection, supervision, or colleague collaboration.

Already we are assessing the person, the situation, and our own skills: indeed, a lot of assessment happens *in situ,* and we are not aware of it as a formal process. However, little assessment can take place unless we can meet the child 'in the moment'. While visiting Chicago, RD Laing was asked to examine a young girl who was diagnosed as schizophrenic: she was sitting naked in a locked, padded room, rocking herself. Laing, to the surprise of the staff, removed his clothes, and sat with the girl in the cell, rocking in the same rhythm. A little while later she began to speak for the first time in many months (see RD Laing's website).

Creativity in Assessment

My own work in assessment is with children in a variety of settings. Obviously the approaches I use in day-to-day therapeutic work contrast with the more formal requirements of assessment for a case conference or clinical meeting, for example. But, whatever the setting, I always involve creative methods that may include: sculpting with stones, shells, small toys ('spectrograms') to explore how the child sees their life or situation. You may find it useful to see the child's family tree, eco-system or world view, through drawing or painting. You can also explore these images through sandplay, with small toys, or other sculpting materials. In Chapter 7 there is the Mandala Diagram, which can also be an assessment tool for discovering the strengths and vulnerability of the child. You may choose to work with, and build up, the strengths of the child, rather than focus on the vulnerability.

Most of the media that you have in the story room – for example, masks, puppets, landscapes, clay models, and pictures – can be useful for assessment. The questions you are asking are 'How does my life look now?' and 'How would I like it to look?', or 'This is my story now' and 'This is how would I change my story', or 'This is me' and 'This is me one day'. Be aware that children may not articulate their feelings in a clear and concise way, and may not verbalise the images that they are painting or sculpting. Assessment is about trying to understand 'where the child is at', within the play or therapeutic or healing space. This space may be symbolic or actual: we may have to create it in the moment, or it may be contained in the story room.

My own philosophy of assessment is to try to discover the strengths of the child, in order to try and build greater health, rather than focus exclusively on the difficulties and perceived damage – I do not use the word 'problem'! For example, when children are feeling very vulnerable, it is not denied or dismissed, but they are sometimes able to recall a time when they felt less vulnerable. They get in touch with some strength, and remember that they have felt better. We are assisting a child to get in touch with their own resilience and capacity for survival.

Resilience is our self-stabilising means of dealing with trauma and crisis, of meeting the world in ways that cope with adversity reasonably. Recent studies of resilience have been based on healthy or adaptive development in the face of stressful situations, rather than using 'disturbance' models. (For a brief history of stress and coping, see Lahad, 1992.) Children have different ways of meeting the world, and a method that can assess coping skills will enable intervention to take place that builds on their strengths and things that are familiar to them, rather than imposing a system on them. Six-part story making (6PSM), analysed by BASICPh, gives an indication of a scale of strengths, through which we may assist someone develop their coping strategies in a crisis. The method given below is taken from the work of Lahad (1992, 2000).

Six-part Story-making Method

You will need paper, and coloured pens or pencils. Explain to the child that they are going to create a story about a hero or heroine, and whether they can achieve the important task they have set themselves. They do not have to be good at drawing: the important element is the story. First the child will divide the piece of paper into six sections of equal size – they may choose to fold the paper into six, or draw six boxes. Then work through the following six stages of the story, one at a time, encouraging the child to draw or write their idea of what happens in each box. The child can take as much time as necessary, and ask any questions as they go along. It is important that you repeat the instructions rather than prompting.

The Six Sections

1 In the first section, draw the hero or heroine, who is the main character in your story, and where they live. Add any words you need, if you wish.

2 In the second section, draw a picture to show the task or mission that this character has to fulfil, or describe it in words.

3 In the third section, draw the character who helps the hero or heroine in their mission, or describe the character in words.

4 In the fourth section, draw a picture to show who or what is the obstacle to the hero or heroine achieving the goal of their mission or describe it in words.

5 In the fifth section, draw a picture to show how the main character deals with the obstacle, or describe this in words.

6 In the sixth section, draw what happens next: does the story continue, or is there an ending?

Now invite the child to tell you the story in their own words, using their pictures as an illustration of what they are telling you. You will need to listen in several ways:

- What tone of voice does the child use?
- What is the context in which the child tells the story?
- How near or far from the story does the child seem to be?
- Is it a reworking of a well-known story in their own words, or does it have significant variations that you need to pay attention to?
- Is it a completely new story that has come out of the child's imagination?

Write the story down as the child tells it to you. and then read it back to the child to make sure they feel you have got it right. The analysis of the story is based on the following scheme, known as BASIC Ph:

- Belief: Are there expressions of a belief system in the story?
- Affect: What feelings are expressed, if any?
- Social: Are there other people in the story?
- Imagination: Has the story an imaginative context?
- Cognition: Does the story contain thinking or concrete facts?
- Physical: Does the story include a physical solution or activity?

Belief

Note down when there is a strong sense of a moral code or right and wrong, or if God and the angels are the helpers – for example, 'Jim is determined to do what is right, and not help the robbers'.

Affect

Are there strong feelings being expressed in the story, by the child or one of the characters? Is there more feeling than thought? For example, 'Mary is so angry at being stopped from winning her prize that she tears her new dress'.

Social

Are the other people in the story an important part of the action? Do they help the main character to achieve the goal of the mission? For example, 'Mary called her friends, and they came and rescued her from her bedroom so she could win her prize', or 'Zack knows he can achieve this on his own – him alone'.

Imagination

Are there magical solutions or flights of fancy? Is the story an imaginary situation rather than being set in real life? For example, 'Ali sat down and wished that he could go up the magic mountain'; or 'Sara was sure that the fairy could help her, so she closed her eyes and made a wish'.

Cognition

Are the thinking processes dominant in the story (often instead of the feelings)? Is the solution very logical? For example, 'Meg knows that the hospital is nearby, so she starts to walk there for some help', or 'Louis made a plan to steal the map from the shop so he could find his way'.

Physical

Does the main character use physical strength or skills to achieve his or her goals? For example, 'Lea pushed the boat out to sea, and sailed away on her own', or 'Sam leaped up in the air like a superhero, and jumped from roof to roof'.

By reading through the story you can see in which areas the child is strong – for example, there may be no feeling, but a lot of thought and belief. In this case, thought and belief are the child's coping strengths, and you start with them, rather than trying to make the child 'express their feelings' or 'be more sociable'. Alternatively the child might rate very high in imagination and physical categories, and less so in the others, so again this is where you would start your story work and play.

You can feed back to the child the strengths that they have shown in their story, and affirm the positive qualities that they have written about. You can also compare the results of the story with observations that you and other people have made about the child: you may get a quite different picture of the child from a parent than the one that appears in the story. Remember that you can also use the BASICPh, Six-part story with adults and with other members of the family. It can be helpful for them to hear each other's stories, and for them each to appreciate similarities and differences.

Assessment Through Embodiment - Projection - Role

In Chapter 4 we examined the developmental paradigm of EPR. This paradigm can also be used for assessment when we observe children during the earlier sessions of play and story work. Assessment through EPR is written up in Jennings, 1998 and 1999; you also need to be aware of Courtney's Developmental check-list in Jennings, 1998. Remember that assessment through Embodiment – Projection – Role, focuses on the playful attachments and resilience that develop through playing. This is essential to the child's healthy maturation, as well as forming a basis for future relationships.

The following chart enables you to record the different activities in which the child is engaged, in their play and stories. It is important to use the chart over more than one session in order to eliminate the effect on the child of the newness of the situation, and apprehension about coming to see yet another stranger. From this chart you can discern which activities the child is engaged in and make them the basis of your stories and play. You can repeat the assessment every three months if you are seeing the child regularly.

Embodiment-Projection-Role Observation

Child's name	Observer			
Session	**1**	**2**	**3**	**Recommendations**
Date				
EMBODIMENT				
1 Touch, Eye-contact				
2 Spatial Awareness				
3 Working With/Against				
4 Whole Body				
5 Body Parts				
6 Body/Self-Image				
7 Mimicry/Innovation				
8 Other				
PROJECTION				
1 Sand/Sand & Water				
2 Clay/Plasticine				
3 Pencil/Crayons				
4 Paint (Finger/Brush)				
5 Single Image/Whole Picture				
6 Single/Large Toys				
7 Environmental*				
8 Other				
ROLE				
1 Body Movement/Gesture				
2 Sound/Speech				
3 Mimicry/Innovation				
4 Brief/Sustained				
5 Relationship with Another Role				
6 Role Development				
7 Scene/Situation Development				
8 Other				
GENERAL OBSERVATIONS				

_____

_____

_____

* houses, dens etc,
with boxes and fabric

_____

Assessment Through Ritual and Risk

The following chart enables you to plot the proportion of ritualistic play and the proportion of risky play that the child undertakes over more than one session. This enables you to plan a balanced programme for the child, rather than re-enforcing 'all risk' or 'all ritual'.

Ritual

Social rituals are shared, artistic or cultural experiences, which are part of our family or community expression. Usually these are to be encouraged as a way of affirming the child's identity. However, children who are referred for being at risk often display isolated ritualistic behaviour, such as rocking repetitively, teeth grinding or self-harming in a patterned way. Examples might include the child who pulls out her eyelashes in a rhythmic way, or creates magic ceremonies around her eating disorder. We would describe this behaviour as ritualistic and therefore dominant in ritual.

Risk

Some children seem to live life at high octane all the time! They take enormous risks with their personal safety, and have no in-built monitor that informs them of risk – there is no internal voice that stays 'Stop' or 'Slow down'. Observe this behaviour, and try to gauge if this is usual behaviour, or if it is being put on specifically for your benefit. Children may use equipment inappropriately, climb on to high ledges or window sills, swing from door frames, or race round the room so fast that they could harm themselves on furniture. This behaviour you would certainly describe as dominant in risk.

When you agree your contract and ground rules with the child, you need to address issues of personal safety, and care of people and equipment. This contract can form the basis of the way in which you work with the child. The Ritual and Risk Assessment Chart allows you to see the balance of repetitive ritual behaviours and risky behaviours. Both ritual and risk need to be part of a healthy creative programme of stories and play.

Ritual-Risk Observation
(Colour in your observations)

Child's name _____ **Observer** _____

| Early in Session | Late in Session |

SESSION 1

Date _____

Ritual | Risk   Ritual | Risk

SESSION 2

Date _____

Ritual | Risk   Ritual | Risk

SESSION 3

Date _____

Ritual | Risk   Ritual | Risk

RECOMMENDATIONS

_____

_____

_____

_____

_____

Assessment with Masks

The masks shown in the pictures on this page form part of a set of 'mood masks' that I use for assessment. These sturdy masks are attached to sticks, and can easily be held in front of the face without children feeling they cannot breath, while still allowing them to speak freely. The masks are designed to show the primary feelings: anger, misery, happiness and fear.

The child chooses to express the feelings of the mask by saying, 'In this mask I am feeling …'. There are also some blank masks, with which the child can create different feelings if they so wish. These feelings may include: feeling depressed, low, down, cool, boiling, or guilty. The masks give you ideas about how the child is feeling, the emotion being projected through the mask. The masks can then be used to create and enact characters for the child's stories.

Many children cannot articulate their feelings, and the mask creates some safety and containment. It is most important to keep to the convention that if you are exploring the feelings of the mask, or the mask's character, then you need to stay with that: it is not appropriate to change the questions to personal feelings – for example, 'Is this how you are feeling?' The child will tell you how he or she feels when they feel secure and confident. However, there may be some things that can only be expressed through the mask.

Common-sense Assessment

With all these charts and methods, remember the initial hunches and intuitive feelings that you had about this child. Have your first impressions been substantiated? Or have you got a quite contrasting view? It is important to record all the impressions you have gained from others, as well as your own, to make sure that your view is not skewed. Create a chart of all these perceptions for yourself. Draw the child in the middle of the sheet of paper, and then add arrows coming into the centre from all the different people who have an opinion. How does it look now? All these perceptions have some relevance, even if they tell you that there has been some prejudice. The following example shows the kinds of perception you may wish to record.

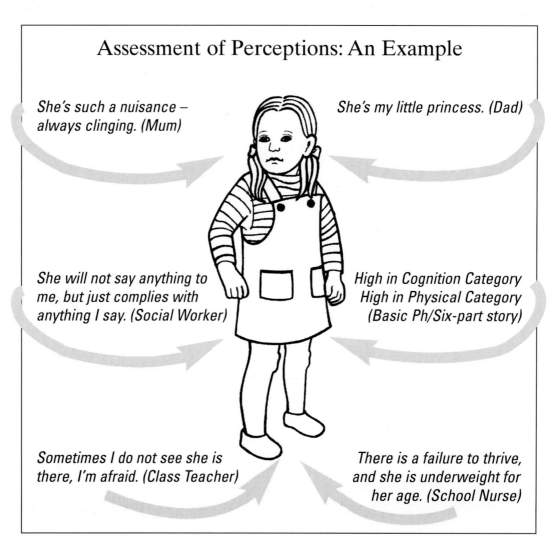

Assessment of Perceptions: An Example

She's such a nuisance – always clinging. (Mum)

She's my little princess. (Dad)

She will not say anything to me, but just complies with anything I say. (Social Worker)

High in Cognition Category High in Physical Category (Basic Ph/Six-part story)

Sometimes I do not see she is there, I'm afraid. (Class Teacher)

There is a failure to thrive, and she is underweight for her age. (School Nurse)

What are your own thoughts about this child, now that you see these different perceptions? How might you start work with this child? Let's reflect on your own practice again, and the storywork that you will be starting: at the end of the day there is a real child who needs your assistance, a child who is at risk. How are you going to start?

Telling Your Own Story

It would be interesting for someone else to do the Six-part Story with you, to see if you agree with the strengths that show through in your stories. Do you agree with the result? How do you feel, now that you have read about assessment? You may feel very daunted, and perhaps you wonder whether you will measure up as a storyteller and play worker. It will keep happening, this feeling of your work overwhelming you and wondering what you are doing. This is where the choice of the right supervisor is so important: when working with children at risk, you need a supportive and objective supervisor who believes in a creative way of working with children. Supervision is important whether we are working as therapists, teachers, or play workers. Perhaps the following story will inspire you in your own creativity.

> Cailleach Beara is an ancient British goddess of creativity, education and knowledge. She is a hag and a wise woman, but is extremely strong. She carries boulders in her apron, and gives shape to the landscape. She lets loose the rivers and makes them flow; her waterfalls cascade in torrents, and the streams rush down the hills. She waves her hammer over the grass to make it grow, and the flowers flourish through her energy. She renews her youth endlessly as her husbands die, and she seeks a new, young love.
>
> Cailleach can give us back our strength and help us think about the bigger picture when we get drawn into unnecessary minutiae.

Find or create a new story for your story-book that you can read to yourself when the going gets tough.

> Let me find clarity in the chaos, and patience to understand the chaos of others.
> Let me not be scared when I do not understand and cannot see the way forward.

Example of an Agreement for Permission to Share Material Professionally

ROWAN STUDIO

Therapeutic services through Play, Drama and Creativity
Research into: Embodiment–Projection–Role (EPR)

Date _____

AGREEMENT

Between _____ *(child's name)*

_____ *(parent or guardian's name)*

_____ *(therapist's name)*

This agreement gives permission to _____ *(therapist)* to include the creative work of _____ *(child's name)* in her research, publications, or talks to professional groups. This agreement covers drawings, photographs of work, stories, and descriptions. The agreement is made on the condition that the work is presented anonymously, and identifying factors are removed.

Signed by all parties concerned

Child _____

Parent/Guardian _____

Therapist _____

CHAPTER 6

Stories and Games For Our Senses

Introduction

THIS CHAPTER DESCRIBES THE importance of our senses, not only in our own development, but also in the development and survival of the human race. The finely tuned skills of sight, sound and smell, together with touch and taste, were, and maybe still are, essential for people to be able to live in harsh and wild environments. We look at simple social games to diminish children's fears – line and circle games contribute to both primary development of the child and other sensory experiences – and create the idea of Sense Boxes. We create the Sense Tree through Embodiment – Projection – Role, which allows stories to be expressed and affirmed.

Although we talk mainly about the five primary senses, it is helpful to consider that there are other qualities that are also referred to as 'senses' – for example, a sense of self, a sense of place, or a sense of time. All five primary senses are part of a totality of bodily or physical senses. When we are exploring the senses through play, we may find that children have other ideas about their senses; but it is important for children to be able to differentiate between their senses and their feelings. Children have different stages and time frames in the development of feeling and senses, and one is needed in order to develop the other.

After many centuries and generations along the evolutionary path we are in danger of destroying our sensory systems, or finding them in overdrive and reacting inappropriately to certain stimuli. It is well documented that children without sensory stimulus from interactive relationships fail to thrive. It is not enough to hang a mobile of moving pictures over a pram, or prop a feeding bottle or play a musical box. Similarly, it is unhelpful to place children in front of computer games, videos, or the television as a means of stimulus, play or creativity. Human involvement and interaction is essential in the early years, in order for our senses to function and develop in appropriate ways.

For the teacher, carer, or therapist, the totally passive child can produce all sorts of feelings of frustration: we may even think about shaking the child in order to get a response, and feel a sense of failure if our efforts are not recognised or responded to. Make a note in your story-book if any of these descriptions produce a reaction in you – you can return to it later. In contrast to the passivity of the child who fails to thrive, there is the child who has too much energy and cannot sit still, or who uses the energy destructively. All these children may not have established a sensory relationship with a caring adult: essentially, we are talking about a sensory relationship that is based in bodily communication, the Embodiment aspect of EPR development, described in Chapter 4.

'He does not know where to put himself', or 'She is beside herself' are phrases commonly used when energy has gone beyond acceptable limits. Both those phrases are extremely interesting if we look at their deeper meaning, and are connected with self as well as identity. The child who is very confused about their 'self' will set up a chain of reactions in us, and these reactions will construct a particular 'identity' that will become reinforced through yet more adult reactions. It is important not to confuse notions of the self with understanding of identity. If I do not know where to put myself, or am beside myself, then I am confused and not in my rightful place, or not in a place where I feel safe and secure. I am discharging physical energy, which often involves the expression of frustration: spitting, shouting, hammering and breaking, self-harming through cutting or bruising, and other similar disorganised or chaotic behaviours.

Again, we can have our own reactions to these children and young people, and their behaviour can arouse angry and violent feelings in us. If we are physically attacked, the situation needs very specific handling. However, we can also be 'beside ourselves' if we are unable to find a meeting point with a child with Extreme Energy Expression (EEE). Perhaps we can note any reactions in our story-books, take a deep breath, and read on!

As we have already seen, many story structures and games have a sensory content that allows the individual child, and children's groups, to continue developing their senses. Physical co-ordination and control, alertness, attention, collaboration and co-operation are all elements of games, many of which have a simple story theme. These games contribute to children's experience of a sense of fun, a sense of belonging, a sense of self, and a sense of time and space.

Simple Games and Scenes

Hide and Seek

This is usually one of the most popular games for children, unless it has been part of a destructive game where children have experienced real fear or abuse. It is possible to find ways to 're-play' the game in order to make them safe again – by playing it with puppets first of all, before you and the child play together.

Tea Parties

Most children who come to play groups or playtherapy, as individuals or in groups, are starving hungry! So much energy is expended during a child's waking day, especially if they have super-action, and they are usually very thirsty as well. A snack of biscuits and juice is often a good settling-down activity while the child is preparing for the play session. (Remember to check for any allergies and special dietary requirements.)

It may be that refreshments are part of the sensory play as a child lifts a spoon of sandy water and invites you to drink, or invites you to join in a scene at a meal table.

It is important be aware of the many different issues and skills that are being negotiated and developed in such a tea party, which are crucial for child development. The ritualised tea party may be in complete contrast to the chaotic meals that the child has at home. The child is developing very fine motor skills in arranging the party. He or she is also practising routines, and anticipating the sharing of food as a pleasurable experience. There is order and a sequence of events that, in themselves, can create order and calm.

One child in therapy has a chocolate bar and a carton of fruit juice every day, which are consumed in the car on the way to school. The child and the parent both accuse each other of never being up early enough to have breakfast together at home.

When we are planning our programme of games, or introducing them in therapy sessions, we need to take care in relation to the child's previous experiences. We need to be alert to the fact that children at risk may have particular reactions to certain games, words, or phrases. For example, 'I'm coming to get you' is usually part of harmless, lively playing; but for some children it can be absolutely terrifying because they have experienced an abuser actually 'coming to get them'. Footsteps outside the playroom, the words 'secret' or 'special', and games of chase are all typical examples of play that can produce distress. This is because the boundary between playing and reality has been broken, and will take time to repair – indeed, for some children it can never be repaired. We must always bear in mind that seemingly harmless material may well cause deep distress in certain circumstances, and we need to be alert to possible signs of this. The example of the Story Map in Chapter 6 is a typical situation where scary images have been internalised and have contributed to nightmares.

Let us now consider traditional games that can assist in developing the senses, as well as co-ordination and training of the body, and collaboration with others. There are many books on children's games, old and new, which are listed in the Resources section at the end of this book. Most of the following games can be played with an individual child as well as with a group of children, so be prepared to join in!

Line Games and Circle Games

There are many children's games that involve fine-tuning of the senses. Most playground games, folk dances and singing games take place in circles, emphasising collaboration and co-operation, and the identity of the social group. A few dances, and many games, also use lines rather than circles, and produce a quite different result, as we shall see from the examples that follow.

Grandmother's Footsteps

One person is grandmother and everyone else – even if there is only one other person – creeps up behind her stealthily, trying not to be heard. If grandmother sees anyone is moving when she turns round, they have to start again. Grandmother's Footsteps contains several quite complex pieces of behaviour, as we can see if we separate out the different movements. There is the capacity to move swiftly and silently while grandmother's back is turned, and the ability to stop instantly as she is about to turn round. We also need the skill to stand balanced without moving a muscle, until grandmother turns away again, and to accept when we are seen moving and have to start again. The game encourages children to practise their sensory and movement skills.

What's The Time, Mr Wolf?

This game also involves creeping up behind someone, who is Mr Wolf, and calling out 'What's the time, Mr Wolf?' Mr Wolf turns round and calls back a time – 'two o'clock', and so on. This continues until Mr Wolf decides to call out, 'Time to eat you up', and chases everyone, trying to catch at least one person. If someone manages to creep all the way to Mr Wolf without him turning round, then they change places. So again we have the capacity to travel swiftly and silently, to react instantly to Mr Wolf, and also to chant in rhythm as a chorus. There is also the thrill of pursuer and pursued in the chase.

These are 'story games', where there are ground rules and an outcome, the senses are activated, and there is a ritual quality of repetition. The shape of the movement is linear, as we are practising individual skills, and need to be able to travel in straight lines without bumping into other people.

Here We Go Round the Mulberry Bush

This is just one of a whole range of circle games, which contrast with the line games by emphasising group participation rather than individual skills. The group skips round in a circle singing 'Here we go round the mulberry bush, the mulberry bush, the mulberry bush; here we go round the mulberry bush on a cold and frosty morning'. Then each person takes it in turns to show an action, which the rest of the group copy and repeat – for example, 'This is the way we stroke the cat, stroke the cat, stroke the cat; this is the way we stroke the cat on a cold and frosty morning'. The actions can be random or based on a theme. Themed games could be based on animals ('ride a horse', 'feed the birds', 'walk the dog', 'hide from a tiger', 'milk a goat', 'step over a snail'), or the morning routine ('wake up', 'get out of bed', 'wash my face', 'dress for school', 'eat my breakfast', 'clean my teeth', 'put on my coat', 'go to school'). Themes can be discussed before the game is played. It is a group event, involving the senses with physical co-ordination and mimicry, where children learn how to collaborate with each other.

Some of the singing and action games involve gender stereotypes, which we need to avoid. 'The Farmer's in his Den' assumes that the farmer is a man, that he wants a wife, and that she wants a child. Historically this would have been appropriate for some sectors of the community, and would have laid out the social rules for particular expectations of family life. However, there have been enormous changes in our attitudes and choices, and these need to be reflected in our willingness to change the words. New words and rhymes can be created, preferably with the involvement of the children themselves.

The circle games, like the line games, are 'story games', but in this case the story has a happy ending. Therefore we could say that the line games prepare us for the world outside, and allow us to practise the fine skills and senses that we need to encounter and deal with danger. This is in contrast to the circle games, which ritualise a set of events and allow us to practise certain skills within a story framework.

The Sense Box

The equipment in your play room can include several boxes and containers which may lead to storytelling. Create a box with different sensory experiences. The simplest Sense Box could include a small rattle, a woollen glove, a little spinning top, a lavender bag and a wrapped chocolate. It is important to allow time for these to be explored, maybe with the eyes closed, if that feels safe for the child. The box itself can be explored, if it is made of wood and carved, and it could have a distinctive wood smell. The contents can all be natural objects, such as an acorn and cup, a seed pod which makes a rattley noise, a piece of bark, a mushroom and a small stone. A simple story can be woven into the exploration of a treasure Sense Box and what it contains, with questions regarding where the object was found, and who put it there. Read the example below, then create your own box, and fill in Story Sheet 6: My Squirrel.

Once upon a time a little squirrel decided to hide some things in a beautiful box. The box had funny lumps on it, and the squirrel, whose name was Squidgy, put into it something to eat and play with when she was lonely in the wood.

This Sense Box, which started off as a stimulus to develop the senses, has already moved into a story that perhaps says something about the child who is telling it. Our reaction may be to start asking questions, such as 'Why is the squirrel lonely?' Please do not change your style of communication into direct questioning about personal feelings: the child has probably begun to share some personal experience and is communicating it symbolically. Therefore, any response you make also needs to be symbolic – for example, you may want to ask 'Who else was living in the wood?', or 'Where did the squirrel put the box?', or find other ways to add to the story. If the child says 'Nothing else happened', or 'That's the end', they must be respected. The child is creating the boundaries, which we need to affirm: the session started off with an exploration of the senses, and that is how it needs to continue; otherwise we are challenging the very safety that the child is creating.

Story Sheet 6
My Squirrel

Name _____ Date _____

The squirrel is called _____ , and it hides things in a beautiful box. This is the story of the box:

_____

_____

_____

_____

_____

_____

_____

_____

_____

P This page may be photocopied for instructional use only *Creative Storytelling* © Sue Jennings 2004

Children can also make their own sense boxes using objects in the play room. This can then become the basis for a guessing game, 'What is in the box?', between you and the child. Children may need a lot of exploratory time with your sensory materials, especially if they have been deprived of this type of stimulus, or feel anxious about making a mess. Finger paint, sand and water, clay, Plasticine, Playdough, gardening and nature play can all be useful. You cannot skip the sensory stage, or children will forever have a distorted experience of the world around them. The development of their senses creates a firm foundation for development of healthy attachments, as well as resilience.

The Sense Tree

Trees can stimulate the senses in many ways: the bark is interesting to touch and smell; the fruit is exciting to smell and taste; you can hear the rustling of the leaves, or the cracking of the branches, and you can see the habitat trees provide for other creatures. The tree has roots, a trunk, branches, flowers, and fruits: and in many ways mirrors the human body. We can use the image of the tree to create stability and growth in our own bodies. The Sense Tree in Worksheet 8 can be explored through Embodiment – Projection – Role, as we shall see in the following exercises.

The Tree of Life

Stand firmly on the floor, with your feet a shoulders' width apart. Bend your knees, and lower your head as far as is comfortable, and then curl your arms round your head. Imagine that it is the end of winter, and that you are a tree with roots reaching deep into the earth. They bring all the goodness from the earth up through the soles of your feet into your body. Your legs, trunk, shoulders and neck are all beginning to grow upwards and outwards. You can grow into whatever type of fruit tree you choose. Spring has come, and there is a slight breeze as your leaves and flower buds appear, and the branches slowly sway. Summer arrives, and there is plenty of fruit: your branches are very heavy as you try to stand upright and reach towards the sun and the sky. Summer turns into autumn, and you are shedding your fruit: some is harvested, some is taken by birds, and some falls to the ground and is neglected. Some fruit has never developed, and drops onto the earth, eventually returning to the earth. It is the end of the autumn, and the tree is bare of fruit and leaves, and slowly goes back towards the earth again. The roots stay stable in the earth during the time of winter, waiting for the arrival and growth of spring once more.

This Embodiment exercise allows the child to 'be' the tree, and feel the stability of the roots and the successful harvest. It creates a cyclic story, rather like the circle story games, where the end returns to the beginning again. The exercise also takes the child through the seasons, and will help to develop more stories and metaphors. Having embodied the story, the child is more able to experience different senses, which can then lead on to a Projective exercise including drawing or painting the tree.

> Because this exercise is similar to the Feeling Tree exercise in Chapter 7, it would be easy for the senses to slip into the feelings. Try to keep the child focused on the senses, building on the earlier sensory play you have shared. Remember that it is through the senses we learn to express our feelings.

Just as we shall be talking about emotional intelligence, we need to acknowledge the importance of sensory intelligence. We know that the central nervous system receives information from the senses. Temporary or permanent damage to the senses, can affect not only a child's affective and social development, but their cognitive development as well.

Now that you have worked with the idea of the Sense Tree, through the body, and then through drawing and painting, it is time to consider the third stage of EPR development, and to try some dramatic play of stories that have derived from the Sense Tree. Look at the picture of the Sense Tree in Worksheet 8 with the child, and explore it further. Having put the different senses in various parts of the tree and coloured them, the child can be invited to think of a story that grows out of this tree. Perhaps the senses are connected to some animals that live in, or at the base of, the tree. Who has a home in the tree? Squirrels, birds (especially a woodpecker or an owl), a snake, a nest of bees? All these creatures can have sounds and senses, and be a part of the child's story. The story can be enacted through puppets that the child makes from paper or card. The story can be dramatised, with you and the child taking on the different roles. Allow the child to be the director, if possible.

> 'I smell a rat, I see a cat, I stroke its fur and I hear its purr.
> It loves to drink milk'
> Donna's sense-poem, using all five senses.

Telling My Own Story

See if you can recall any sensory memories from when you were a child – for example warm towels when you got out of the bath, the smell of a certain food being cooked, patterns and shapes in the branches, the taste of your favourite food, the sound of reassuring voices. Maybe some of your memories are less positive, and there were cold rooms and shouting voices. Write these early experiences into your story-book and keep a balance between positive and negative memories.

Draw your own Sense Tree and use it as a starting point for a story, using lots of metaphors and descriptions. Which of your senses is underused? Which of your senses is not cared for?

Give yourself a treat of things that smell or feel good – lavender? velvet? What do you really savour the taste of? Go for a walk in a landscape you really enjoy – what can you hear? Allow positive memories to live in the present, and write or draw them all in your story-book.

Worksheet 8
The Sense Tree

Name _____ Date _____

The Sense Tree becomes a tree that grows
different senses: they become the fruit, and
maybe even be the roots.

Speechmark P

CHAPTER 7

Stories for Feelings and Emotions

Introduction

MANY OF US WORK with children who have difficulty in managing and expressing their emotions in age-appropriate ways. The frozen or watchful child gives nothing away, and often provokes increased violence from others because of this. The over-exuberant child, who goes beyond all reasonable limits in physical and verbal expression, both towards people and surroundings, attracts the idea of medication 'just to calm him down', or 'to help her help herself'. The child who will not stop crying and screaming, and often clinging, tests our patience when nothing we can suggest seems to work. Parents, foster parents, care givers and teachers, all know these situations: child psychotherapy or play therapy are sometimes seen by truly desperate adults as the only alternatives to medication. Therapy, and indeed medication, may be the answer. However, I think that it is important to consider some strategies along the way, especially as extreme behaviour has usually gone on for some time before drastic action is seen as necessary – someone cannot cope any more, so something needs to be done in a hurry, often through an emergency case-conference.

If a child is deemed to be 'at risk', it is important to build in some play interventions early on, before the behaviour, and the adult coping with it, reach crisis point. In this way we can do much more preventative work, and find new ways of communicating and playing in order to transform the challenging behaviour. Unfortunately, we are often asked to deal with a crisis intervention, which is usually not in the best interests of anyone concerned.

> Children will always give you clues as to the 'where' and the 'how' they need to work.

The Lifeline

You will need a large sheet of paper, crayons, coloured pens or pencils and a drawing pencil. Take time to introduce the idea of the lifeline. Link it to stories about the past and the present – for example, 'When Mary was a baby, she lived in a house that …' (as you make up a story), or 'A poor woodcutter lived at the edge of a wood with his two young children …' (as you read the story of Hansel and Gretel). Talk about the past, the present, and the future; yesterday, today, and tomorrow. Talk about, and draw, roads and paths: straight ones and winding ones, those in the country and those in the town.

Now invite the child or group to create the path or road that is their own life. How far back can they remember or have they been told about? Suggest that they can draw where they came from, all the way to where they are now. Children will usually produce roads or squiggly lines with various objects or signposts along the way. The process may awaken a range of feelings about the road, which will sometimes include indications of barriers or blocked 'no go' areas.

Bringing the lifeline up to the present can lead to the child being able to take more control of what has gone before. There may be stories to tell, scenes to be played out, or action to be taken, if you find that a child has disclosed something for the first time. There may be favourite times and unhappy times, and the child can be helped to deal with the unhappy events by being able to recall that there were also good things. The Lifeline technique can also give a feeling of continuity, in which one thing has led to another; and, having arrived at the present, the path may be different for the future. A future 'wish' line can be drawn for the story that the child would like to have, an important extension to the activity when there are uncertainties in the present.

It may be that the child has completely blocked off the past, and will only relate to the here and now – phrases such as 'I can't remember anything', 'Just tell me what you want', or 'School is awful and I want to change' are typical, and should be acknowledged. You cannot push the Lifeline technique: you can only invite its use. You could use the Story Map, described below, and work in the present and the future; or work with fears and feelings in their immediacy; or use fairy stories, myths, or television dramas, as described in Chapter 9.

The Story Map: The Child as Pilgrim

We are all familiar with the phrase 'Life is a journey': indeed, it is probably overused as a metaphor, and we need to re-engage with its meaning for our therapeutic and remedial work. I was reminded of the idea of the 'Healing Journey' (Jennings, 2004) when I was asked to work with a group of children on the theme of Pilgrimage at one of the ancient abbeys. We discussed why people went on a pilgrimage, and the children came up with the following suggestions:

- To say thank you for something.
- To say sorry for something.
- To ask for something for somebody else.
- To ask for something for yourself.
- To ask for healing for yourself or someone else.

All the children arrived in costume as medieval characters, including soldiers, monks, nuns, rich people and poor people, and those with various wounds and crutches – I think Chaucer would have been proud of this group! They all had to choose one reason for going on a pilgrimage. The reasons given were many and varied, including: 'I want to ask for help for my big sister because she is nervous about her exams'; 'My mum is ill and I want her to get better'; 'I want to say I'm sorry because I've killed somebody: I'm a murderer'. (The latter child said, a little while later, 'Miss, I've changed me mind: I've broken my leg and I want it to get better'!) This drama exercise enabled many children to express deep-seated anxieties. There were several children who were extremely concerned about a member of their family, for reasons which included illness, unemployment and examination worries. The drama project that set out to be an educational, historical exercise, also included a lot of pastoral care, and expression, 'through the role', of issues that concerned the children.

It was this experience that gave me the idea for Story Maps – the idea of life journeys, and the child as pilgrim. Therapeutic play work enables movement for the child who is stuck in a situation: it can be inner emotional movement, or actual, physical movement. Whatever the starting point for the movement, it will enable psychological movement for the child, just as the extreme movement of the over-active child can be seen as a desperate attempt to discover more appropriate movement. People may well be familiar with the idea of a child drawing a lifeline to represent their journey through life: where they began, and important events on the way up to the present, using pictures or signposts and other indications of whether the journey twists and turns or is direct. The Story Map is similar, but has the idea of creating a context for the lifeline, so that children are able to tell stories as they re-visit their journey.

The equipment and preparation for the Story Map is the same as for the Lifeline technique. The child draws the line or path as described above, and you introduce the idea of a landscape or surroundings. You can prompt with questions, such as 'Is there anything growing near this road?', 'Is there some water?', or 'What is the view?' You can say to the child that the path is part of a map, and perhaps there are signposts, which give directions. Perhaps there are animals or other symbols to indicate what stories are happening along the way. The creation of the Story Map may well take a whole session, as the child develops more confidence to fill everything with paint or crayons. The idea of the child as a pilgrim on a journey will create a sense of movement, which is especially helpful if the child is feeling very trapped.

The child can then choose which story to start with (the choice does not have to be sequential), and tell it with symbols and drawings, or with words and metaphors. You can introduce the idea of a companion for this journey of re-visiting the past, such as a toy or puppet that the child chooses. It may be that the child chooses the puppet to tell the story while you listen. It is important that you do not interrupt: you should only speak if the child stumbles and looks to you for help, if there is extreme emotion and the child cannot continue, or if the child is so stuck that the story also becomes stuck. Any intervention must stay within the context of the story, as the story is a continuous process. For example, if the squirrel is telling the story, then a question could be, 'And then what did squirrel do?', or 'How was squirrel feeling after this happened?', rather than direct personal questions addressed to the child. The two examples below demonstrate the process.

Thomas' Story Map

Thomas is eight years old, and very angry. He creates a very straight road with lots of traffic on it and no turnings off. There is nothing in the landscape on either side. There is no vegetation in sight. I ask him about the traffic, and he says that all the cars are driving very fast and that he is in a tank, so he can shoot anyone who gets in his way. I ask him if that is his map now, or if it has it always been the same picture: he replies that he cannot remember anything else, and that is how it is now. Trying to keep within the road idiom, I wonder where the next filling-station is and whether the tank has to get to the army camp. Thomas then asks for a bigger piece of paper, and places his map in the middle of it. He then draws a fort with gates and guards outside, and a road leading to it. He also draws a garage with petrol pumps and a café. This movement, from the smaller map to the larger one, seems to give him a greater sense of freedom. He then begins a story about the soldiers being very strict at the fort, and how the tank would escape and shoot everyone in its path. At a later stage, we are able to introduce the idea of stopping in the café for a drink, and thinking about what else the tank would like to do. Slowly, Thomas begins to create the possibility of a different path – and, therefore, a different map.

Jenny's Story Map

Jenny is six years old, and has come to see me because of nightmares. She seems fearful, and looks in wonder round the play room. I introduce the idea of the Lifeline and the Story Map, and she sits at the table and starts to draw. Her line is very winding and intricate, and she draws lots of trees and bushes. There are signposts saying 'danger', and when I look closely at the trees I can see that there are eyes staring out from them. Jenny chooses one of the small squirrels, who is her companion on the journey, and the squirrel tells a story:

> Squirrel says to the little girl, 'Do not go into the woods because there are lots of wild creatures who will come and get you. The monsters have got big eyes and teeth, but if you stay on the path and do not wear red, then they will not notice the little girl'.

Two things immediately strike me when she tells this little story through the squirrel: first, some details are compressed from the story of 'Red Riding Hood'; and second, perhaps the tale *Where the Wild Things Are* might just be helpful. Yes, she had heard the story of the little girl who goes into the forests and meets the wolf, but she did not 'know' the second part of the story. I suggest that she finds a way to have something like the squirrel at home, which could tell her about any dangers that might be on her path. Meanwhile, I make a note to consider working in dramatic play with her fear story, or perhaps to let her take control of the monster through externalisation methods, as described by Marner (2000).

Worksheet 9
A Story Map

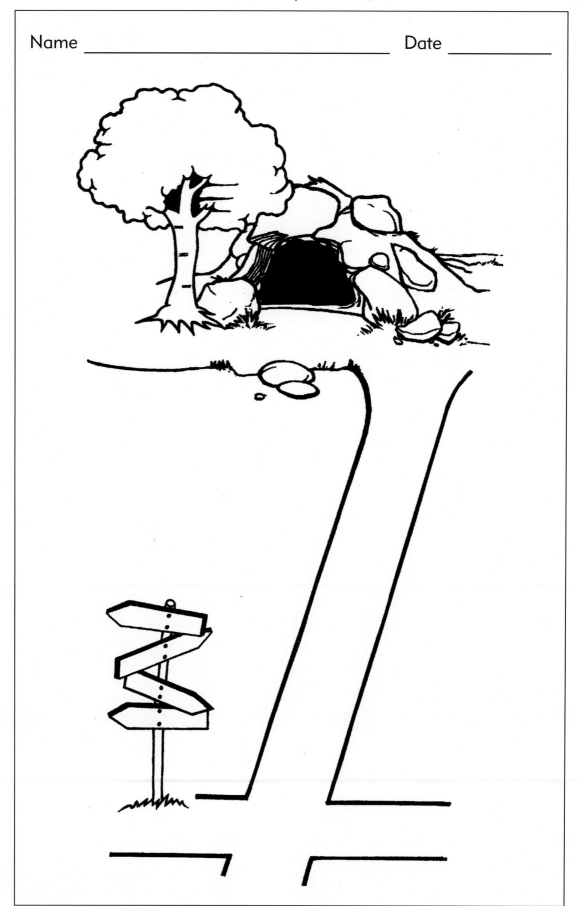

Name _____ Date _____

Worksheet 10
My Story Map

Name _____ Date _____

Stories and Circles

Circular symbols occur in many cultures: the dreamcatchers and medicine wheels of the Native Americans: rose windows in cathedrals and churches; spirals and mazes, and, of course, the mandalas of Far Eastern cultures and religions. All of these circular patterns can be used in our work with children, and help to create a sense of wholeness and inclusion.

The Dreamcatcher

The dreamcatcher is a very important symbol for allowing fears and nightmares to be expressed, and for enabling positive, practical action to be taken in future. I have bought dreamcatchers for all my grandchildren, and we have also told stories about them, and about Grandmother Spider who lives in the centre of the dreamcatcher. A dreamcatcher can be a hoop of any size, made from wood, metal, or leather, with a web woven across from side to side. There are also beads woven in which represent Grandmother Spider. She filters all the dreams, gobbling up all the nightmares, only allowing pleasant dreams to come through. There are many stories about Grandmother Spider, including her creation of the alphabet (Jennings, 2004). You can also link the dreamcatcher with a real spider's web – see whether you and the child can find one: it is especially magical if covered in frost or rain. Stories and poems can be created about a spider's web.

You can buy dreamcatchers from 'alternative' shops, make them yourself, or make one with the child. The child can hang special toys, photos, or other precious objects on the dreamcatcher. This can be a variation of 'life story' work, where the child is able to acknowledge important people and objects with the dreamcatcher. The child can also paint a dreamcatcher, and create Grandmother Spider from clay or Plasticine. I always have one dreamcatcher hanging in the story room where I work with children, which acts as a starting point for story and dream work. The following picture of a dreamcatcher can be photocopied, and coloured in by a child or a group.

Story Sheet 7
My Dreamcatcher

Name _____ Date _____

My Dreamcatcher Story

Grandmother Spider sits at the centre of her web

_____

_____

_____

_____

A Dreamcatcher Story

Many years ago, a white buffalo was born to a Native American tribe: the Native Americans believed that this was very lucky, and that they would have good fortune. However, one of the children of the tribe was very exhausted. She never had a good night's sleep because she was always waking up, thinking that a giant buffalo was trampling through her wigwam as he thundered over the plain. Sometimes she heard the noise of hooves in the distance, and this added to her fears. Her grandmother noticed how tired she was, and guessed that it was because she was suffering from sleeplessness. Instead of asking her direct questions, grandmother told her the following tale, next time she said goodnight to her:

'Grandmother Spider was very worried about the children of the tribe: they were looking too pale, but she knew they were spending a lot of time dancing and singing every evening. All the adults were having celebrations because the weather was good, people had stopped fighting, and the Pipe of Peace had created a good calm.

'The adults were dancing, and their feet pounded the ground as they danced the Buffalo Dance, hour after hour. The children copied them, and tried to dance too, waving their ribbons, and calling until their throats were hoarse. No wonder the children are tired, thought Grandmother Spider. She decided to send the Mist to cover the Plains, and a great sleep came over everybody. They slept for a day and a night, and then everyone woke up refreshed and strong. The children knew the sound of the feet dancing and the sound of the buffalo hooves, and were unafraid. They would dance again to celebrate the White Buffalo, but not every night: they would keep it special. The dance of the new White Buffalo would bring good fortune to everyone, especially the children of the tribe.'

The Mandala Method

The word 'mandala' comes from the Sanskrit word, meaning 'whole' or 'wholeness'. Ancient mandalas are sacred paintings, and tell epic stories and philosophies. Personal mandalas can help children to tell their stories, and also to find strengths and skills in order to deal with their fears.

When working with adults, the segments of the mandala are labelled as follows: 'Who or what guides me?'; 'What are my skills?'; 'What makes me vulnerable?'; 'How am I creative?'; and 'What do I believe?' There are variations (see Jennings, 1998 and 1999), and the technique can be applied in training, adult therapy and supervision.

Adult Mandala

In work with children, the mandala needs a different language – a language that is accessible for children, and that is age-appropriate. For example, the segments can have the following questions that the child responds to, either through words or drawings or both: 'Who or what looks after me?'; 'What am I good at?'; 'What am I scared of?'; 'What do I play at?'; and 'What do I believe in?'

Child Mandala

Invite the child to complete Worksheet 11: My Mandala. Once the child has drawn and written on the mandala, they can then explore it in different ways. The segments can then form the basis of stories, but the important thing is that each of the segments balance the other. For example, the child who is scared can be supported by their guide, or whoever looks after them; and the child who feels they are not good at things will find strengths in their play.

I was working with a group of children, together with their teacher, who said that she thought the exercise was too difficult and that the children would not understand it. She was very shocked to discover that one girl wrote in her Fear section that she was scared of her father. When she told her story, she said that her father would throw a bucket of cold water over her when she had an epileptic fit. Another girl drew a picture of a smiling face in her Fear section, and said that she was scared of her father when he got drunk. The teacher asked her to say more about the smiling face, and the girl replied 'That's me, and I am feeling happy: my father is in prison now'. Mandalas can be used for assessment, in order to find the right starting point for the child, and can also be repeated after several sessions, when any changes can be discussed with the child.

Worksheet 11
My Mandala

Name _____ Date _____

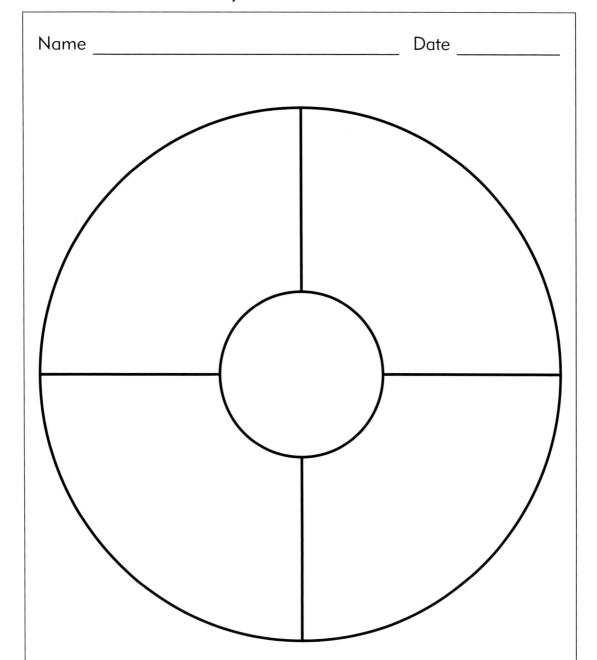

My Mandala is about who cares for me, what I'm good at,
what I'm scared of, what I play at, and what I believe in.
I am learning that

_____

who cares for me understands my fears.
I am getting strong enough to overcome my fears.

Umbrellas and Clouds

The child who is fearful or ever-watchful needs to find some experience of safety, whether it belongs to the past, the present, or the future. The Umbrellas and Clouds technique can assist the child to acknowledge some of the darkness, while, at the same time, feeling some safety. The umbrella can have a name, belong to someone, or have a quality, just as the clouds can also have names, qualities, or belong to specific events in the past or the present. The clouds can be rain clouds, so the umbrella can be protective; but they can also have sunshine emerging from behind them. The three pages of Worksheet 12 will help you to work through this activity with the child.

I usually start with the umbrellas, discussing the way in which they protect us from rain and storms, and invite the child to name and colour their umbrella. The children may feel they have more than one umbrella, and that some belong to the past, and some to the present. You can then progress from the protection of the umbrellas to the darkness of the clouds. You can use the pictures on the Worksheets to colour in, or encourage the child to draw their own clouds. Again, allow the child to name the clouds if they are ready to talk about their experiences.

You may wish to do more preparation for this exercise, and precede it by talking about different sorts of weather, and the ways in which the weather affects how we feel. Do we feel happier when it is sunny? Do we feel sunny outside but miserable on the inside? What sort of weather is like our inside feelings? In this way we are assisting the child to find metaphors to express their feelings. If there are very heavy cloud pictures you can then explore how to find a new umbrella, and tell the story of how it is found. The Umbrella and Cloud technique is one for you to play with and find different ways of using. Children themselves will also contribute with their ideas, and tell stories about their 'weather companions'. The technique is less confrontational than many 'feeling' approaches, and gives scope for the development of the imagination. It is also a useful technique to use near the beginning of your play work, in order to see what issues the child may be ready to explore.

These are specific techniques for working with feelings, but many ideas in other chapters can also be useful. It is important to remember that many children do not have access to, nor do they have the language to express, their feelings – hence the whole development of the field of 'emotional intelligence'. Through stories and play, and the use of metaphors, children will develop the pathways to express themselves. In time, they will often be able to acknowledge their feelings in age-appropriate ways, and have a repertoire of creative means to give shape and form to chaotic and destructive experiences.

Worksheet 12a
Umbrellas and Clouds

Name _____ Date _____

My special umbrella to keep me safe

My dark cloud that I need to change

Worksheet 12b
My Umbrellas that Keep Me Safe

Name _____ Date _____

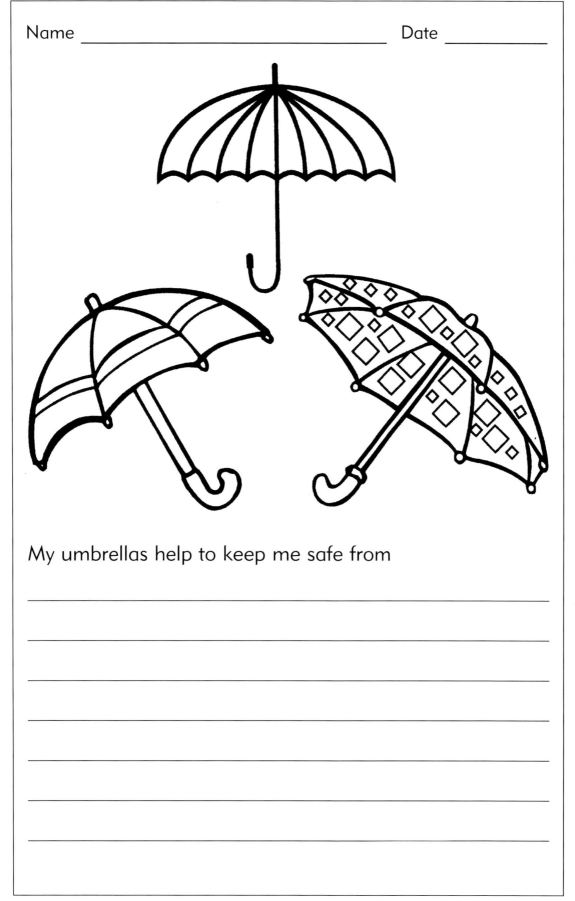

My umbrellas help to keep me safe from

_____

_____

_____

_____

_____

_____

Speechmark

Worksheet 12c
My Clouds that Make Me Feel Unhappy

Name _____ Date _____

I am going to change my clouds by

_____

_____

_____

_____

_____

_____

_____

The Feeling Tree

Through the Feeling Tree technique, the child is able to begin the process of accessing their feelings in a structured and contained way. As we acknowledged earlier, children's emotional intelligence depends on their having not only sensory experience, but also being able to express their feelings appropriately. Often, if you ask a child how he or she is feeling, they will answer neutrally or dismissively, or treat the enquiry as a social question – 'How are you doing?' will often be answered with 'Fine. What about you?' In play and playtherapy, we are demonstrating that the language we use can sometimes belong to various social conventions, and the child or adolescent may be unclear as to what we are actually demanding. Usually, the fewer the questions the better: instead, find opportunities to explore feelings and issues.

The Feeling Tree is similar to the Sense Tree of the previous Chapter 6, but it allows the child to express him or herself at a great depth, and with more differentiation. Therefore, deep-seated feelings can form the roots, strong feelings the trunk, and the many and varied feelings that we experience all the time can be the fruit of the tree. Once the tree has been created it is possible to look at the feelings that the child wants to change. The tree can contain all the expressible feelings, as well as the feelings that are too large or overwhelming to be otherwise safely expressed. Stories and games can be created that enable these feelings to be explored in different ways. Worksheet 13 will help you go guide the child through this exercise.

This story tells us a great deal, symbolically, about the girl who created it.

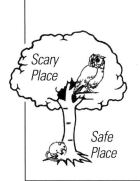

The Scary Owl Story

Inside the tree is a big owl that can see in the dark and hunt small animals. He chases the squirrels away if they come too near. A little mouse with a silky coat lives in the roots, but she is a bit scared of the owl, because she might be eaten. She goes out when the owl is hunting.

Worksheet 13
My Feeling Tree

Name _____ Date _____

I have many
different feelings
MY strongest feelings
My deepest feelings

I have many different feelings.
Some of them scare me. Some of them I have lost.
Some of my feelings feel too big for me.
I can express my feelings through playing.

Feeling Cards

You can create a card pack by copying the individual apples printed on Worksheet 14 on to cards. The child can write and colour different feelings on each apple. You can do the same, and the activity becomes a game, where you and the child compare your words and pictures. Try making two packs, and play 'snap' with the child. You can turn the cards with the pictures face down, and each person takes a card at a time and expresses the feeling on the card for the other(s) to guess. The expression can be physical with no words (embodiment) or with words (role). Several cards can be used to create the characters for a story or for a dramatic scene.

Simon 'coloured' his life in the following rhyme:

'Life is green, life is grey, I'm going away, so I can't stay'

Worksheet 14
Feeling Cards

Name _____ Date _____

Cut out the cards. Colour in the pictures to show different feelings, and write the feelings on the lines.

Telling My Own Story

There are many pictures throughout this Chapter that you could choose to draw or to write a story about. Looking through them, which one appeals to you most? My favourite is always the dreamcatcher: I have made, drawn, and painted dreamcatchers for many years, and have also created group dreamcatchers with colleagues and friends. I am fascinated by the stories of Grandmother Spider, and the practical advice she gives to the native Americans. The Pollen Song is one of Grandmother Spider's chants to which you can dance, or create your own picture.

The Pollen Song

Put your feet down with pollen

Put your hands down with pollen

Put your head down with pollen

Your feet are pollen

Your hands are pollen

Your body is pollen

The trail is beautiful

Be still

If you read the chant through several times, you will find the rhythm starts to get hold of you, and you can tap your feet or clap your hands. It is an action chant, but it also says 'Be still'.

CHAPTER 8

The Child's Story

Introduction

IT IS IMPORTANT FOR us to remember that the most important aspect of storytelling is for the child to tell their story. Can you remember when your story was never listened to? This Chapter describes in detail stories that children have brought to the story room and have told through different forms of playing, including sandtray work. The metaphors in the stories speak for themselves, and enable the child to create very powerful images that could not be articulated in any other way. We must stay with our 'not knowing', because then the child will tell us what he or she needs to tell.

The child needs us to hear the story they have to tell, and we must be able to listen to it. The story may be told in many different ways, and through different materials, but the 'story relationship' that we have with a child will mean that we listen with utmost respect. For example, it is not helpful if we leap in and finish sentences, or pre-empt an ending. Even if we think we know what a story is about, we need to listen in a neutral way, otherwise we already have its 'meaning' worked out in our heads, and will lose what the child is really trying to tell us. Because we are always searching for meaning, and ways to understand the people with whom we work, it is easy to lose our total attention to what we are being told. We are not only are listening to the content of the story, but also noting the way it is told, the tone of voice, the gestures, and the body posture. For example, our reactions are very different if a story is told in a flat voice with no light or shade, and no indication of feelings. We might then consider the ideas later in this Chapter for developing the voice.

It is very helpful to the child if we feed back the story as we heard it. We should not interrupt the story, unless it is going off in so many directions that we need a pause for reflection. Try to wait for a natural break or a natural ending – you can then say, 'Let's see if I have got this story right', or 'Let's make sure that I have remembered the story'. This will clarify the story for you, and affirm to the child that you have really listened. Listen to the child if he or she corrects the story: as we find, time and time again, children are often 'not seen and not heard'.

The following story is told through sandtray work by a nine-year-old girl, who has been several months in playtherapy. She has witnessed extreme domestic violence, and has to 'mother' younger siblings. She comes to playtherapy because 'she is anxious, loses her temper and, at times, is unmanageable'. She will talk about her feelings, and seems desperate for some normality and calm. She is always polite and grateful, and at times talks to me as an adult, inquiring after my health, and commenting on the décor. She self-harms by pulling out her eyelashes, telling me that she does that when she feels cross.

She tells me that she loves drawing. Children have the freedom to start with whatever they want from the choices in my story room. It used to be called the playroom, but I changed the name to appeal to all age groups. I make sure that a range of drawing and painting materials is available for her. She initially chooses charcoal, but then changes to pencil and creates pictures of formal houses and landscapes, which she then paints. She paints in a very controlled way, mixing colours until they are just right and using a range of brushes to get the desired effect – all very focused Projective work. This lasts for several sessions until we talk about her having her own box to put her things in, and she decides to decorate the box both inside and out.

She starts painting with the finger paints, but uses a brush, so I ask her whether she would like to use them as finger paints. She looks at me and says, 'I haven't done that since nursery school', and proceeds to paint her hand with the finger paints. This makes her very frustrated, so she scoops some paint and presses it between her hands. Unexpectedly, for her, it makes a 'farty' noise, at which point she bursts into endless child-like giggles – the first time she has laughed since coming to see me. So now she is quickly finger-painting her box in order to have more paint to make 'rude noises'. It is clear that she is now in the Embodiment stage, having been in very controlled Projection. She is slowly becoming more relaxed as her play is less controlled, and her sessions are a combination of Embodiment and Projection, combined with a little storytelling, but she is not yet ready to take on roles. Although she has talked about the masks, she does not want to 'do drama'.

The following is her first story. She creates patterns of creatures in the sandtray, and then tells the story as she moves the creatures around. She wants me to write her stories down as she tells them, so I type them up for her by her next session, when she reads and, if necessary, corrects the text.

Story 1

Once upon a time there was a wicked old hag. She took the beautiful fairy princess of Avela, and took the mighty treasure of King Bartholomew, and also his beautiful twin daughters, Helga and Thelga. She imprisoned them in a fortress, with evil dragons, a dinosaur, and two fearsome gorloks and a phoenix.

Many brave men and women tried to rescue them. They tried to cross over the bridge, but none could get past the phoenix. Others tried to swim across the moat, but the place was heavily guarded with gorloks and fearsome dragons. Others met with the witch herself, and were doomed as a toad in the murky marsh.

One day a group of friends, a phoenix, three centaurs, and two warriors, went to rescue them. The phoenix destroyed the phoenix, and helped destroy the dinosaur and the dragons, not to mention the fearsome gorloks.

They poisoned them, struck them with spears – kicked them – and set fire to them on the bank – and then with their swords went to rescue the princess. They killed the hag – breathed fire on her – stabbed her from behind – slashed her with a sword – and kicked her. They returned the girls – returned the treasure – and the warriors married the twin princesses – the phoenix finds a mate and the centaurs do the same. The beautiful princess finds a handsome prince in the fair land of Avela. The treasure is returned to King Bartholomew.

We can see how the story starts in a conventional mode of a fairy story about 'goodies and baddies'. There is no hope for the captured princesses, as the wicked hag proves stronger than all the rescuers. They could not get over the bridge, nor cross the moat, and those that did were turned into toads. It is a group of friends, rather than an individual hero or heroine, who is able to overcome the forces of evil. It is the good mirror image of the baddy that finally overcomes the evil: 'the phoenix destroys the phoenix'. Good finally triumphs over evil, and the ending has everyone getting paired off and married, even the animals. It is a utopia where everything is normal in a very conventional way.

Between the conventional beginning and ending is the most fearful destruction. It is important to understand the level of anger and violence that is expressed in the attack on the old hag when she is killed: she had fire breathed on her, and she is stabbed 'in the back'; she is slashed with a sword, and then kicked. To be kicked after all these other gruesome fates seems quite child-like, after the extreme adult anger. However, this little girl also has a very descriptive skill with her use of adjectives and metaphors – which leads us on to the healing power of metaphors.

The Healing Metaphor

The healing metaphor in drama, poetry, and stories is one of the most powerful agents of therapeutic change. To express ourselves through metaphor means a move from the left hemisphere of the brain to the right hemisphere. The left hemisphere, through logic, science, mathematics and rationality, dominates Western education and culture, whereas the right hemisphere is involved in communication through play, the arts, and symbols. The free-flowing play of young children often turns into the formal exercise of schooling. Sometimes I ponder on the fact that the young child with special needs who has access to a nurture group or play therapy is able to continue to play, whereas the child without difficulties often has to adhere to a more formal regime. The following stories show a constant use of metaphors, which seem to help express some very extreme feelings for this girl. The second story has different characters and settings from the first, but some of the themes are very similar. However, its mood is very different from the first story.

Story 2

Once upon a time there was this village, placed in the faraway land of Cava. By the village there was a great hill, and no one believed its name. Some believed that there used to be big land, because the hill was massive – others said that it was just a nonsense, but still wrote the legend of Atlantis.

One day a little girl called Susan walked past the hill on her way to school, and saw all these things sticking out of it: bits of wings, feet, tails, manes, fences sticking out of the hillside. She ran to get everybody else in the village, and they called a meeting. The monk said 'The legend of Atlantis is true.'

Suddenly, a load of fearsome creatures popped up from the soil, and started moving towards the villagers, and a huge land appeared that had been buried under the sand for millions of years. The beasts and other strange creatures took over the village, and ate all the children and the women. But the men, including the monk, saw their chance to escape, so they did.

The beasts and other creatures took over the land that was once theirs, and ate whoever crossed their paths. And that was not many, because the men and monks had told them, and everybody had heard the warning, and fled to distant lands. The beasts forever roamed that land.

The tone of this story is very different: there is a feeling of hopelessness as the fearsome beasts win over the humans. The men, with the monk, run away, and the women and children are eaten. Scary bits and pieces pop through the hillside before turning into creatures, so we are warned what happens when scary bits start breaking through. There is a sense of inevitability by the end: people have either been eaten or have run away, and the monsters now rule. Note how the writing has a rhythm to it, as if the rhythm and the metaphors are needed for the story.

I decide on this occasion to offer a story to this child, which she readily accepts. We need to create some balance, and allow the possibility of containment to exist. The monsters have taken total control, and the women and children have all been eaten. When you offer a story it can be based on the story that the child has told you, with a variation, as in the example below, or it can be another story from a fairy tale, or a newly created story. Whichever it is, it needs to carry important metaphors for the child to hear. On this occasion I thought it important to empower the little girl, Susan, who first discovers the fearsome bones sticking up through the hill. There is also some folklore, introduced as a mirror image of Susan (the mirror image is one which the child herself uses in her tales) where she can have some fun and take part in dancing rituals.

My story for the girl

Well, there were more things happening in the land of the monsters where the people were so frightened – everybody was terrified of these enormous devouring creatures. Fear was everywhere. However, Susan, who had first seen the bits of the monsters half buried in the sand, was determined to return, and have another look at the hill. Was there anything she had missed because everyone had been so fearful on that dreadful day? Susan crept back and searched the landscape, and yes, there was something – so small that she had missed it. There were some rocks on the hillside that concealed a small cave. She decided to investigate, and crept inside cautiously, scared that there might be another monster in hiding there. She sat down and tried to accustom her eyes to the dark, and when she could see a little, what a surprise!

There were no monsters, but the most amazing pictures covered the walls – pictures of this village in the olden days, many, many years ago. There were people in the village going about their daily lives, looking after animals and doing their washing. They were also celebrating and dancing round a big fire in the village square – there was a wonderful feast for everyone to share. And Susan saw that there was a little girl, just like her, in a colourful costume, dancing to the drum – she was very happy. Another painting showed a monster coming towards the village, but the villagers were not frightened: they were very strong, and stood up to the monster. They did not run away. Susan was puzzled, and wondered why everyone now was so scared of these creatures. What had changed?

She realised that she had been away quite a long time, and that her mother would be worrying about her. She crept out of the cave, made sure that the entrance was concealed with the bushes, and then ran home as fast as she could. She would come back again and find the answer to her quest, so that the people of the village would not have to live in fear.

The third story seems to be a continuation of the second, as if this is the next episode.

Story 3

The dinosaurs went to sleep for a couple of hundred years. When they woke up, they found themselves on this desert island, with two small pools and two palm trees as shelter. They all started moving towards the pools and shelter – they were all very thirsty and very hot. As they approached the shelter and the pools, they realised that they might have to work together to get off the island, which was out of their nature. They called a meeting, and decided to dig and see if they got anywhere. They dug, and dug, and dug, until finally they found the land they came from and fell asleep in. Although on the surface no one noticed it, they had dug just one hole and it still looked like desert.

The dinosaurs in their own land were happy and content, and started to get their natural lives. And they were never discovered and still live there now. They breeded, and became huge like before – before they had slept so long that they became small dinosaurs – and eventually they grew back to their natural size.

There is a theme in this story of 'leaving well alone, and everything will revert to normal'. The dinosaurs found their own land again, but they needed to co-operate in order to achieve this. They became their normal size and lived natural lives: they were also never discovered.

The fourth story continues the narrative. It is linked to the dinosaurs, but is also a tale that brings in some new humans, who have survived a shipwreck.

Story 4

A couple of thousand years later, in exactly the same desert the dinosaurs had disappeared from, two cabin boys and two servants survived a fearsome shipwreck. They were friends, even though none of the crew liked them. It was a pirate ship.

As there were lots of trees on the island – big palm trees and stuff – and quite a few pools of water, and quite a few sources of food, they decided to build their own little raft. They took a couple of buckets of water (the buckets they had been using for cleaning the ship), and some bananas and stuff, and coconuts, and set out on the long journey to another small island nearby, populated, of course .

They built the raft in five days, and collected the food, and were off. Eventually, after many hard-going days at sea, they saw a small little island populated with the most friendly people. Once they found out the island's name, and found that the people were really friendly, they decided to settle by the sea. The happy little island they had come to was called Hawaii, and they raised families, generations after generations. They lived happily in peace and harmony for thousands of years.

The humans who were not liked by the crew nevertheless work together to build a raft, and go on a 'long journey to another small island nearby' – an expressive metaphor indeed! The island is populated by friendly natives, and they raise families. The peace and harmony is obviously very important. This story coincides with a plan for the girl's family to move to the seaside where there are very friendly people.

The fifth story is the longest, and takes us through several scenes and complex relationships.

Story 5

Then something happened, after thousands of years, in the quiet isle of Hawaii, that changed its history forever. On an ordinary summer's day, the inhabitants of Hawaii saw strange objects land on the sand of the beach, and the chief went to inspect the strange animals that had arrived on their peaceful beach, and wanted the others to stay back in case they were dangerous. He asked some of his best warriors to come and guard the things that had landed, and his bodyguards protected him. The chief inspected them and thought they were harmless and dead. Just as he and his soldiers and bodyguards turned their backs to declare they were harmless, the creatures attacked.

The people were terrified, and ran away in fear, and fled the island to several other small islands nearby. They warned them not to approach the once harmless, beautiful, harmonious and peaceful island of Hawaii. Many did not believe them, and disregarded their warnings, and went to see if it was true. None of them returned, and gradually the people started to believe the old inhabitants of Hawaii. The creatures had invaded and made the island their own.

One day a group of brave warriors declared that they were going to try and fight the monsters who were inhabiting Hawaii, and reclaim it. In a small, very carefully armed boat, they approached the island, and, to their horror, found that the monsters had breeded, and were no longer just monstrous, namely spider, snake and monkey, but monkey-snakes, monkey-spiders, and spider-snakes, as well as a few of the original monsters. They had almost completely destroyed the island – it was totally changed, and only a mere shadow of what the island once was. There were bones scattered all over the place, remains of trees poked up through the sand, and branches here and there. Huge snake skins lay amongst the scattered bones and the branches. The island was devastated.

The warriors thought to sneak up on the fearful monsters in the dead of night and slay them. They crept up on the animals, and slaughtered three-quarters of them, until they realised that the rest of them were awake and alert, and lurking in the shadows, ready to repel and eat them if they came too close. The soldiers realised this, and quickly ran to the nearest cave. They thought the cave was deserted at first, and ran straight in, but soon realised that three of the monkey-spiders were lurking in there, ready to repel and destroy them. They quickly jumped up and, with their swords, killed them. The warriors were terrified that they had managed to destroy three of the most powerful monkey-spiders with only a few scratches left on them to prove it. The monsters were so scared they did not realise that the warriors had sneaked up behind them, and, with a signal, slayed them. There were so few monsters left that the warriors could slay them all at once. They went back to tell the others of their success, and the people who dared went to live there happily ever after.

The monsters are back, and again lie buried or scattered on the ground. The chief gets it wrong, and we should listen to the old inhabitants who know about these things. The lovely utopia is destroyed. This time, however, the warriors decide to fight back, and reclaim the island. They use stealth to creep up on the monsters, and succeed in killing them. However, there have been mutations that create even more scary animals; but the warriors win through, and even the monsters are scared. Those people who have the courage go back to live there happily ever after.

The girl's next brief story takes us on a different journey with disastrous results.

Story 6

One of the brave adventurer's ancestors made a journey to England, to settle down and have a family. Little did he know that there was a great plague in England at this time. They got into the ship to England and sailed off.

When they reached England they found a beautiful countryside before them, and wished to go to the City of London. After a large search, they managed to find somebody who would take them to London, because many would not. When they arrived they saw many parts of dead people, and they were very shocked because no one had told them about the terrible plague that seeped and ran through the streets of London. The Black Death was a terrible disease carried by rats, and could kill you.

They thought that most of England was like London, and sought transport to get back to the port, to get away from this dreadful land.

This was the last story for several months, as the girl switched her activities to making clay figures, masks and drawings. It is very brief, and quite horrific, with the 'terrible plague that seeped and ran through the streets of London' forming one of the most powerful uses of metaphor in all her stories. However her main character also has a sense of reality, and manages to get to London and to get away again.

This sequence of stories illustrates a child's progression through two months of play therapy where she wishes to keep telling stories. It occurred after six months of work with other media, and suddenly took over as her only means of communication. The stories illustrated the actual past and current events in her own life, which were so painful that they need archetypal figures and metaphors to express them. The girl was also finding her own strengths through these different characters. The world can be treacherous, with things not being what they seem and creeping up on you unexpectedly. The fearsome monsters contrast with the utopia she longs for. But utopia cannot last; there are always darknesses lurking. However, if people work together, there is a possibility of overcoming the dangers. In these stories it is possible to understand some of the girl's worst nightmares, nightmares of an ever-changing situation that cannot be controlled. Slowly, she is developing some strength, however uncertain the future.

The following story from a child's life history was turned into a play, and performed for her new foster mother.

Rejection: A play based on Katie's life story

Scene 1: At the hospital

DOCTOR: *(With stethoscope.)* Here you are Debbie, a beautiful, strong, baby girl for you!

(Hands baby to Debbie.)

DEBBIE: *(Cradling baby.)* Ah, isn't she pretty: look at those lovely eyes! She's so alert! She's looking all over! *(Doctor leaves the room. Baby is heard crying.)* Oh no, she doesn't like me! Oh, give it a rest will you! (*Quickly puts baby down.*)

SCENE 5: At home

(*Phone rings.*)

TEACHER: Mrs Clay? It's school here again: sorry to trouble you, I know you've a lot on your plate, but the children haven't come to school. Is there anything we can do to help?

DEBBIE: Oh just call the Police, why don't you! (*She bangs phone down, then passes out.*)

(*Knock at the door.*)

POLICE CONSTABLE: (*Calls through letterbox.*) Anyone in? Kids, can you let me in please? (*Door flies open.*) Look at this! She looks dead to the world. She must have emptied the drug shelf at the chemist, judging by the state of her, not to mention the Off Licence! Better take a look at the bedrooms. Good Grief! What's this? No blankets – only black binliners for the children's bedding! What a stink! I don't know what's been going on here, but you kids had better come with me. I know someone who'll look after you 'til Mum's better. (*Dials 999.*) Ambulance to 34 Buttercup Fields, please.

SCENE 6: At School in the Head Teacher's office

TEACHER: Hello: Katie and Ben, isn't it? What's the problem? Ben, did you say Mum won't let Katie live at home? Is that why you brought her bags? Oh dear – well let's ring Mum and see if we can sort this out. (*Teacher phones Mum.*)
Hello, Mrs Clay: Ben tells me that you and Katie aren't getting on too well!

DEBBIE: He's right there! You won't persuade me to have her back – I've had enough! I can't stand it any more! She's nothing but trouble, that one.

She just doesn't fit in with the family, and that's all there is to it. *(Bangs phone down.)*

TEACHER: Oh dear! I'm so sorry Katie. I'll phone Social Services. You'd better go to your classroom while I sort something out for you. You don't need this; it's too awful.

Telling My Own Story

As you read through this chapter, be aware of the images that touch you in the different stories. Which story would you like to know more about? If you have some small toys or objects, place them in a pattern that will let you tell a story about them. Give the story a title. Can you recall not being heard as a child?

I ask the question at the beginning and again at the end, because it is crucial for us, as well as for the children with whom we work. If our story was never listened to, we need to be extra vigilant that we do not neglect the child's stories. Give yourself permission to really hear your own story as you tell it and illustrate it in your story-book. Worksheets 15 and 16 and Story Sheets 8 and 9 will help you and the child with ideas for stories.

128

Worksheet 15
When Dinosaurs Roamed the Land

Name _____ Date _____

Story Sheet 8
The Island Story

Name _____ Date _____

Once upon a time there was an island where _____

_____

_____

_____

_____

_____

_____

Speechmark ℗

Story Sheet 9
My Island Story

Name _____ Date _____

Imagine a magic island. What does it look like? Are there any trees or caves? What creatures live there?

Draw your magic island in the space below, and describe it in a story.

Once upon a time there was a magic island called

_____

_____

_____

_____

_____

_____

Worksheet 16
My Mythical Characters

Name _____   Date _____

Speechmark

CHAPTER 9

Fairy Stories, Myths and Legends

Introduction

WE HAVE HEARD ABOUT myths and fairy stories that can form the basis of our work with children. The stories can be read and shared, but they can also be enacted through drama and dressing up, or puppet play. The stories used are chosen on the theme of the four elements (water, earth, fire, air), and are grouped under a symbol source – the Story Pool, the Story Tree, the Story Cauldron, or the Story Bird. Alternatively, you can choose not to work with a specific element, but use the symbols for creating new stories and re-discovering old stories. The symbols are all infinitely flexible, and it is important to work in the way in which you and the child feel comfortable.

There are abundant fairy tales and ancient stories that contain archaic truths, as relevant now as they have ever been through time. Every culture has its stories, many of which are passed on by word of mouth, others through ancient manuscripts, and yet more from the central part of the sacred lore of different cultures. There are stories in our folklore tradition as well as in our sacred books, and they all need our attention. However, as we found with the games described in Chapter 6, there are some stories which were created 'of their time', and that reinforce stereotypes and prejudices which are unacceptable today. These are stories that we need to change or exclude from our repertoire.

We need to have a broad repertoire of stories that we know, and to have studied them in some depth. We do not necessarily need to know our stories off by heart, though the more we tell them the more we will remember them! It is a good idea if we have our own special book or folder in which to record the stories we gather from different sources. We will also have tried the stories out with our colleagues and friends, our children and our neighbours' children, and asked the questions, 'What is this story about?', and 'Who do you think would enjoy this story?' And remember: we find stories in many places, including the places where we go on holiday, and places remembered from childhood, as well as from the internet and the many, many books that proliferate in bookshops, charity shops and markets.

The Story Pool

Many stories have water as a central theme, whether the characters are going on a voyage, crossing a river, or finding a magic pool. The Story Pool is a symbolic representation of a container of stories, and in this chapter we shall use it as a container for stories about water. You and the child can write down all the stories that you know about water. Put them all into a blue pottery bowl, and choose one of them to tell with pictures. You could include 'The Little Mermaid', 'The Voyage of Odysseus', 'The Frog Prince', 'The Lambkin and the Little Fish', 'The Nixie of the Mill Pond', or 'Jonah and the Whale'.

One of the watery stories in my Story Pool is the ancient tale of the nine daughters of the sea goddess Atargatis. It is a story of 'looked after children', stormy journeys, and new lands and homes. There are images in this story that can be drawn and painted, or modelled, such as the many-coloured egg, the stormy sea, the caring doves, and the safe leather coracle. Here is the story:

The Nine Daughters of Atargatis

Delphine – Alysson – Hermione – Sabrina – Anita – Melusine
Lorelei – Merlene – Undine

In ancient times, in the lands of Phoenicia and Mesopotamia, the ancient gods and goddesses inhabit many parts of the landscape. The beautiful Atargatis is an ancient goddess of the sea who has many daughters. Atargatis is born on a stormy night, out of a sacred egg of many colours. The egg is brought to the River Euphrates on the back of a stormy wind, and laid gently on the turbulent waters. The egg rocks back and forth, and up and down in the rough waters, but it does not break. The egg is kept safe until it is time for Atargatis to be born.

She has the tail of a fish and the body of a woman, with beautiful long, thick, black hair. Immediately she starts to swim through the waters, and all the sea creatures love and respect her. Her special sea creature is the dolphin, and the dolphins follow in her wake, and they play and leap together in the water. Some of the pictures of Atargatis show her with a crown of dolphins on her head.

We shall call her first-born daughter Delphine. Her mother decides she cannot look after her, so she takes her to the wilderness, where she is cared for by doves. Delphine has more sisters, and each time they arrive in the wilderness, the doves care for each one of them.

Soon the nine sisters are able to go and play in the sea themselves, and leap and swim in the waves. They ride the storms together, and sit on the rocks, singing their haunting songs, which carry on the winds to the sailors on the trading ships.

The three older sisters, Delphine, Alysson and Hermione, are growing up and care for their younger sisters. The three middle sisters, Sabrina, Anita and Melusine, can be silly and giggly, and sometimes swim off and hide. The three little sisters, Lorelei, Merlene and Undine, are still quite small, and are teased by their middle sisters. The older sisters sometimes have to stop the playing when it gets out of hand, and remind the sisters that they all have to care for each other.

One day, the older sisters call all nine together to tell them they are going on a journey. It is time to go to a new land, and they are going to follow one of the Phoenician trading ships to the Pretannic Isles, where the waters cover most of Somerset, and there are clusters of islands that can only be reached by leather coracles. The Phoenician trading ships sail up and down the Bristol Channel, to and from the port of Bristol. They bring silks and spices, especially the popular nutmeg, and carry rough and sweet wines and assorted dyes, including the popular cobalt blue. They exchange their goods for tin and bales of raw wool, and sometimes for rough woollen blankets.

All nine sisters – the three older sisters Delphine, Alysson and Hermione, who are sensible, the three middle sisters Sabrina, Anita and Melusine, who can be a bit naughty, and the three little sisters Lorelei, Merlene and Undine, who are growing up fast – lie hidden in the harbour while the three trading ships are loading up. The quayside is very noisy, as the sailors call to each other and check that everything is safely on board. They set sail on the tide, and the nine sisters follow them, excited but a little nervous about their new adventure – the biggest adventure of their lives.

They follow the ships, and play and dance on the waves – then they sing the sailors to sleep, and hold onto the bows for a rest. Each ship has a different figure-head as its mascot, and the mermaids hold onto their necks for the ride.

There are great storms that tip the ships almost on their sides, and the sailors are shouting out with fear. But then it becomes tranquil again, and there is scarcely enough wind to blow the sails. Eventually land is in sight: it is the Bristol Channel, and the three ships skilfully steer their way up to the port. The sailors leap out of the ships, and go to find food and a bed for the night, before starting their hard bargaining with the local Celtic traders.

The mermaids slip silently away, and start to swim across the marshy plains towards Avalon. The sacred apple orchards are beckoning to them, and the nine sisters think they may have found their new homeland. They follow the leather coracles that ply their small trade between the islands of Avalon, and discover the sacred wells and healing springs in the landscape.

The Phoenician traders have long gone back, and the mermaids feel quite cut off from their original ocean home. There are some moments of longing for the old home, but they know there is a new life here. They stay in touch with each other with their singing and games, but they each find their own space – a well or a spring which is their new home. They become the guardians of the healing waters and feel they can settle in their new place and grow with the landscape.

Read the story to the child, and then complete Worksheet 17 and Story Sheet 10, encouraging the child to create imaginative variations of the story.

Worksheet 17
My Mermaids

Name _____ Date _____

Speechmark P

Story Sheet 10
My Favourite Mermaid

Name _____ Date _____

Draw a mermaid and write her story. You might like to choose one from Worksheet 17, or you can draw your own mermaid.

My favourite mermaid is called _____

This is her story of her journey and her arrival at her new

home: _____

_____

_____

_____

_____

_____

The Story Tree

Following my theme of the elements, which started with water and The Story Pool, I am going to continue through the remaining elements of earth, fire, and air, and create structures for our stories. The Story Tree, which also echoes other tree images in this book, represents the element of earth. The tree has deep roots going down into the earth. The earth inspires the tree with many stories about woods and forests, about plants and earth creatures, and the many people who can live in the woods – witches and wise people, woodcutters and forest spirits. The Story Tree can include 'Hansel and Gretel', 'The Poor Woodcutter', 'The Three Little Men in the Wood', 'Jack and the Beanstalk', 'Red Riding Hood' and 'The Laidley Worm'. 'The Invisible Child' is retold below as an example of an earth story from my Story Tree.

The Invisible Child

'The Forest Family are sitting round a table, peeling mushrooms they have picked that day. Outside there is a storm raging and the wind blowing against the windows – it is raining as if the clouds have burst. Their house is in a forest and the wind is whistling through the trees.

There is a tap at the window and the door opens – their cousin comes in, dripping wet, in a large yellow raincoat. 'I have bought you a visitor', she says. 'Who is that?' says Ma. 'You can't see her', says the cousin, 'She has lived so long with her sarcastic, cold aunt, that she is invisible, and her aunt puts a bell round her neck so that she knows where she is'. Sure enough, they could all hear a tinkly sound crossing the room to the fire, and see wet paw prints on the floor. 'I must be going', says the cousin, and she goes into the dark forest night.

Ma decides to prepare a room for the child, and places an apple and a warm drink by the bedside. She lights a candle, and notices a little bump appear under the bed cover and a small dent in the pillow. Not a word is said, and Ma goes downstairs, and sits long into the night, reading Grandmother's recipe book. She is looking for a recipe to make someone visible again. 'If people get misty and difficult to see …', 'Right' she says, and starts to mix the medicine for the new little family member.

The next morning, Ma, Pa and the children notice two little brown paws and the sound of the tinkly bell, come down the stairs. The child takes some breakfast, and then the whole family go out to the orchard. It is apple picking day, and there is applecheese to be made. They light a fire and, as the children pick the apples, Ma minces them and cooks them in her big pot. The child is so excited, she knocks the pot over and spills the applecheese: immediately she becomes invisible again. Ma says, 'If you want the earth to grow something for you, then you have to give it a present, that is what grandma used to say'. Immediately the paws and now the legs of the child become visible. Everyone continues the picking and the cooking until bedtime.

That night, Ma finds her old red petticoat, and makes it into a little dress and hair-band for the child, then leaves them by the side of her bed. The next morning she comes down the stairs wearing her new dress, and she is visible up to her neck. The children decide that she could learn to play games with them and have some fun. It's very hard going as she has never played before and, in the end, one of the children shouts, 'You don't know how to play and you can't get angry – no wonder you have not got a face'.

Days went by and nothing changed at all – a little red dress and two sets of paws, a red bow, but no face. Pa decides it is time they all go on a picnic to the seaside. They all pile into the noisy, bumpy, old car and, when they get there, the children play games on the sand. The child stays near Ma as she sits on the landing stage, dangling her legs in the water. The child turns round and notices with horror, that Pa is creeping up behind Ma and is about to push her into the water.

The child gives a snarl and bites Pa's tail – he, in turn, topples over and falls into the water. Everyone laughs and laughs, and suddenly the very angry face of the child can be seen by everyone. 'Pa was just having some fun', says Ma, as Pa tries to retrieve his wet hat. The child then laughs as she realises that everyone is playing a game.

This is a story that many children and adults identify with. We all know children who are the victims of bullying and violence, sarcasm and silence, who, in the end, become 'invisible'. The love of the Forest Family in the story, and the wisdom in Grandmother's Recipe Book allow, for healing and change. There are many things to discuss and draw. Some children like the apple orchard, others like the two brown paws coming down the stairs, and yet more identify with the bell – the means of being heard. Everyone seems to enjoy the scene of the Forest Family peeling mushrooms that they have picked in the woods, and you could encourage children to colour in Worksheet 17 when they have listened to the story.

Worksheet 17
My Mushrooms

Name _____ Date _____

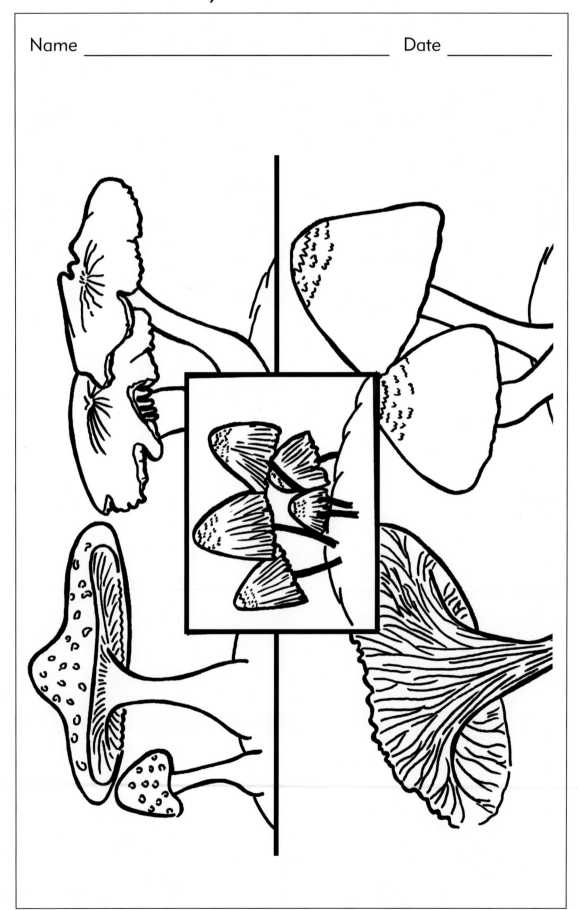

The Story Cauldron

The magic cauldron is bubbling away on the fire, and there are many stories being created in the mix of all the ingredients. Think of all the things that go to make a good story, and put them in the cauldron – witches and wizards, storms and rainbows, ghosts and ghouls, wolves and bears; the possibilities are endless! What other ingredients can you think of? Let your ingredients bubble and simmer, and see which mix comes out in the steam for a story that has fire somewhere in the tale. Good examples are: 'The Firebird', 'The Little Match Girl', and 'The Tinderbox', the last of which is given below. You may like to use Worksheet 18 and Story Sheet 11 with the child to help you to create a story together.

The Tinder Box

Many years ago, a soldier returns from the wars and is marching home. He has a few scratches, but nothing serious – he has his sword in his hand, a knapsack on his back, and not a care in the world. An old witch stops him and calls him a very fine fellow, and asks if he will do something for her which will give him a rich reward. The soldier agrees, and the witch ties a rope round his waist so he can get inside a very old tree and climb down to its roots.

The witch tells him that, once inside the roots, he will see three doors and each one is guarded by a fierce dog. He must place the dog on the witch's apron, and then take as much money as he wants from each room. He must also bring back an old tinder box which has been left there.

The soldier does as he is told, and finds the first door and the dog with eyes as big as saucers. He places the dog on the apron and sees the room full of copper coins, but decides to leave them. The next dog has eyes as big as mill-wheels, and is guarding a room full of silver, and the soldier puts the dog on the apron while he decides whether to have the silver. The next dog is quite terrifying, with eyes as big as suns, but he places him on the apron and sees a room full of gold. He stuffs all his pockets with gold, picks up the tinder box which he nearly forgot, and returns up the rope and out of the tree.

The witch demands the tinder box, but the soldier says that she cannot have it unless she says what it is for. The witch refuses to tell him, so the soldier cuts off her head. He wraps up all his gold in the witches apron, puts the tinder box in his knapsack, and walks into the nearby town. He finds somewhere to stay and buys himself some fine clothes. Everyone in town says that the King is looking for a person to marry his daughter. However the soldier soon spends all his gold, and his new friends who thought him to be a rich man, soon desert him. He has to move into a little dark room which has no light at all, until he remembers the tinder box and strikes a light for himself. Well! He strikes it once, and the dog with the eyes like saucers appears and asks him what he wants. The soldier says that he needs money so desperately, so the dog returns with a bag of copper coins for him. He realises that if he strikes the tinder box twice, the silver dog will come – three times and the gold dog will come. Each dog will bring whatever he wants. He is able to move back into his rooms and wear his new clothes – and of course the friends that like his money also return.

The soldier wants so much to see the Princess who is locked in a copper castle by her father, since there has been a prophecy that she would marry a 'common soldier'. The soldier strikes the tinder box, and says he wants to see the princess – and lo and behold! There she is, riding sleepily on the back of the dog, and she is very beautiful. The King and Queen are sure there is some mischief, so they set an old woman to watch the Princess. So, when the dog brings her again, the old woman marks the door of the soldier's house with a white cross so that he can be found again. However, the clever dog puts white crosses on lots of houses so that no one can be sure which house is the one that the Princess visits.

The Queen is very clever, and makes a little bag with a hole in it, and fills it up with flour, and ties it to the back of the Princess' dress. The next night when the dog takes her to the soldier, there is a trail of white floor all the way to his door. He is arrested by the soldiers and thrown into a dark cell, and told that he will be hanged the next day. In the morning he can just see through the grill at the window, and calls to a passing shoemaker's boy, asking him to fetch his tinder box from the hotel, and he will reward him.

The boy fetches it and the soldier gives him some money, and then he is taken to the gallows for hanging. All the town is there to watch, including the King and Queen on the throne, but no Princess. The soldier asks for a last request – he wants to smoke one pipe of tobacco before he dies, which is a usual request, so the King agrees. The soldier strikes the tinder box one, two, three times, and the three massive dogs appear. They rescue the soldier, chase away the terrified soldiers, and throw the King and Queen and courtiers up in the air, and they smash into little pieces. The people all call for the soldier to be the new King, and he rescues the Princess from her imprisonment in the copper castle. She recognises him at once, and they have a lavish wedding, which lasts for many days, and which the dogs also enjoy. They rule the land in a just and fair way for many years to come.

This is a story of good triumphing over evil, but also about overcoming fear. We have the magic formula of three dogs, three rooms, and three strikes of the tinder box. It is a story of empowerment, and the soldier being able to be as good as the royal family. There is also a theme of the Princess being imprisoned against her will in the Copper Castle.

Worksheet 18
Magic Story Mixture

Name _____ Date _____

Ingredients for a Good Story

Witches and Wizards

Ghosts and Ghouls

Storms and Rainbows

Wolves and Bears

146

Story Sheet 11
The Magic Story Cauldron

Name _____ Date _____

My favourite story in the cauldron is _____

This is how I remember the story:

_____

_____

_____

_____

_____

The Story Bird

The Story Bird flies in from many lands with stories to tell: maybe it has a scroll in its beak, with a new story that has some links with the air. For example, we could have 'The Wild Swans', 'The Nightingale and the Rose', 'The Little Prince', 'The Raven and the Ash Tree', 'Jonathan Livingstone Seagull', and, of course, all the stories about fairies and angels. Here the Story Bird is bringing us rhymes about birds which in themselves are stories.

> One for sorrow, two for mirth,
> Three for a wedding, four for a birth;
> Five for silver, six for gold,
> Seven for a secret not to be told;
> Eight for heaven, nine for hell,
> And ten for the devil's own sel'.
>
> One for sorrow, two for mirth,
> Three for a death, four for a birth;
> Five for silver, six for gold,
> Seven for a secret never to be told;
> Eight for a wish, nine for a kiss,
> Ten for a time of joyous bliss.

We can play these games and create stories from their themes. A child may well be ready to tell the 'story never to be told'; or might benefit from exploring the silver and the gold, or the sorrow and the joy. The stories can be told through pictures, words, or the sandtray. The bird itself enables the child to fly to another land where, perhaps, life is a little more friendly.

Story Sheet 12
The Story Bird

149

Name _____ Date _____

My favourite story about birds is _____

This is how I remember the story:

_____

_____

_____

_____

_____

_____

P This page may be photocopied for instructional use only. *Creative Storytelling* © Sue Jennings 2004

Telling My Own Story

There are many stories about journeys in fairy tales and myths. Can you recall a favourite story from your childhood? Who read the story to you, or did you read it for yourself? Write it in your story-book, and try to recall why it was (and perhaps still is) your favourite story. Has it been an inspiration for you in your adult life? Would you tell this story to other children now? Perhaps you can find illustrations for your story or draw them yourself. Perhaps you can find new stories for your collection from your own culture, whatever it may be – I know that I have neglected my Celtic inheritance for many years. I am inspired by Olwen, who is also called the Lady of the Golden Wheel, or Leaving White Footprints, because with every step she takes a white trefoil grows. I like the idea of flowers growing under my feet!

We close this chapter with a short invocation that includes several elements, and which was written by someone who is very hurt:

The Healing Forest

In a land far away there is an ancient green forest with trees that are hundreds of years old. A river runs through the forest, and animals come down to the river bank to drink. The trees meet over the river, creating a green tunnel, and the river is slow flowing, rippling over the stones and debris.

The forest trees tower in the air. There are layers upon layers of vegetation in this forest, which lie undisturbed. The forest holds many secrets that have never been told, and contains stories of many generations. The river flows on, washing away the wounds as it goes.

Spirit of the forest, hold my story;
Spirit of the river, heal my pain;
Spirits of the nature, witness my life.

CHAPTER 10

Creating Stories Together

Introduction

IN THIS CHAPTER WE shall look at different ways of creating and telling stories with individual children and children's groups. The emphasis is on co-creating the stories, rather than only the adult or only the child being the narrator. The adult may be the prompter for the story and have various starters or props to do this. The stories can be danced or moved (Embodiment), or drawn or painted (Projection), or enacted (Role). The enactment may also lead to a performance. For example, foster parents are able to understand a child's situation when a play worker and child are able to dramatise the child's story to them. The performance of a story takes it a stage further in externalising the child's experience and communicating it to others. The performance maintains the safety and containment, with the costumes and/or masks, and by making the characters vehicles for the child's story.

Moving the Story

The warm-up to a story can be a physical game, or some of the embodiment methods, such as the rolling and resistance, pushing and pulling, or over and under. We can also do the jelly shake and the wubble face, always allowing the child the opportunity to choose a warm-up. Try moving as different animal characters – 'I am moving like a hungry cat: follow me', or 'I am moving like tired elephant: follow me'. You and the child take it in turns to create the animal and follow each other. The child may also ask you to move like a tiger for example, while he or she watches, and you could ask, 'What sort of tiger?' before moving. You could also see if the child will move while you watch. It is important that the animal characters have some contrasts, so that if the tiger is scary, the blackbird is safe, or if the mouse is frightened, the salmon is happy. They have contrasts in their feelings, and in their habitats: water, land, trees, air and so on.

During the warm-up, certain animal characters might appear to be particularly important to the child, and will form the basis for the story, or we may need to prompt and ask which of the animals will be in today's story. The story can be planned with a brief structure, or improvised. Characters can change over, watch each other, or mirror each other's feelings. For example the safe blackbird can mirror the scary tiger's movements, and vice versa. With the movement story, it is important to keep words to a minimum so that the characters can express themselves fully through embodiment. This can be done in several ways:

- When two characters have been chosen, they can move and improvise a story together – for example, 'The frightened mouse and the happy salmon'.
- Plan together a rough outline for the story and give it a title, such as 'The day the scary tiger met the safe blackbird', and then tell the story through movement.
- Swap the roles over and move the story again, perhaps bringing in a new element, such as a journey to a new place.
- Introduce the idea of the animals dancing – and maybe they can dance their feelings to each other and with each other.
- Choose a piece of music to dance the story to, which expresses the different moods and feelings.
- Use scarves and pieces of material to 'extend' body movement.
- Create both movement and sound for the creatures, and practise the different voices.
- Choose mythic creatures, such as Pegasus, the Minotaur and a mermaid.
- Use the same methods to create a story with human characters – for example 'The angry man and the frightened child', or 'The nice granny and the silent child'.
- Tell the story through musical sounds instead of movement.

Telling the Story Through Pictures

Story pictures can be created with crayons or finger paints, charcoal or painting, or in the sandtray with small objects. It is important to do a physical warm-up, even if it is only a stretching exercise while we sit in the chair or on the floor, or rubbing or massaging our hands. The invitation, 'What story shall we tell today?' will usually give a focus or a theme. Remember that in this chapter we are creating stories together, so you may be painting too, or involved in some other way, such as contributing an appropriate idea.

You may both decide to paint the picture that you have been moving to and dancing, or to paint a character from the story. In this situation, children feel safe to express what they want through the stories, which may be about past pain, present confusion, or future hopes. The story does not have to be verbalised, but the invitation can be there, provided there is no feeling of expectation: it must feel all right just to create the pictures, without an obligation of turning them into words. However, some children will verbalise the story as they are painting, or creating the picture in the sandtray, or will want to share the picture with you afterwards.

- Remember to have a choice of materials, including crayons, paints, glitter glue, stickers and several sizes of paper and card.
- Other materials, such as clay, Plasticine, dough, play slime and a sandtray with many small objects, can all be materials for projective storytelling.
- If, for example, the picture is 'The Mess', invite the child to tell the story of the mess, rather than imply that it is his or her messy feelings, which it may well be.
- 'And then what happened?' is a very useful prompt for storytelling, and keeps you involved in the process.
- Paint a story together, taking it in turns to paint or draw something.
- Prompt a story with suggestions such as, 'I wonder what colour the boy's feelings are', or 'Is there anything on the other side of the hill?'
- Several clay figures created over the weeks can be named and become characters in a story.

- If the child is repeatedly creating negative and dark pictures and stories, it is important that these are accepted as they are, without trying to simplify or ignore the feelings being expressed.
- It is also important that the child can see that there is the possibility of change, love, hope, care, which you offer through your presence and, perhaps, a story.
- Always make clear with the child what will happen to their painting – is it for taking home or is there a safe box or file for all their creations?

Tina's Short Story

Once upon a time there was a very bad fairy. She is very cross. She stays in her bed with her cuddly toy, which is a snowman.

Enacting a Story

A story can be improvised, such as 'The Story of The Hungry Hedgehog', or use an existing story, where the child may well choose to be director and actor. Children may want to create specific scenes from their own lives, if they feel safe, and there may be disclosure material that you need to be alert to. Scenes that show 'This is how it is' can be balanced by asking 'How would you like it to be?' One technique is called 'laddering the story': we create the idea of a ladder, the first rung being the story now, and the top of the ladder being what we hope will happen, with the rungs in between representing all the stages from the bottom to the top. This will enable the child to see that there could be a different outcome, as you explore the stages or rungs between the present and future situation – if this is how it is and that is how you would like it to be, what needs to happen, a step at a time, in order for the situation to change? All the steps can become scenes, and can be enacted as people or animals who are part of the story. The scenes might include the child telling the teacher, the teacher telling the social worker, a meeting of the people who might be involved, and so on. It is important that children feel they have a part to play in all this, rather than decisions being made over their heads, which, sadly, is often the case. We still assume that, as adults, we know what is best for a child; however, the child will probably not be so explicit with their story, because one of the fears is that by telling someone else, the child thinks the result will be that 'I will be punished', 'I will be taken away', or, 'I will not be believed'. It is more likely that the very serious stories will be told through creatures, images and metaphors.

- Try to gauge whether the child is ready for storytelling through role, having of course done plenty of movement and projective work in previous sessions.
- If the child has not suggested 'doing drama', suggest that one of the fairy stories could be told with all the actions, and see what happens.
- Always keep a clear closure of any enacted story, so that both you and the child have time to come out of role and be yourselves again, with time for processing the story.
- Be accepting of the story the child chooses to enact and the roles he or she would like you to play, even if this means, 'I'll be the boy, and you be everybody else!'
- Provide simple costumes – cloaks and shawls, assorted hats and crowns, and longer pieces of material that can be fastened with Velcro, all as neutral as possible to allow freedom of expression.
- Have some larger pieces of material available in order to create an environment for the story – for example, blue for water, brown for a cave, and green for the forest.
- Larger pieces of material are also useful if you have to work in a classroom or office: it is a good idea to cover up intrusive furniture, and protect things not to be touched.
- Masks can be placed on chairs, together with a drape of material, in order to create other characters in the story.

The story that the child has to tell, and its changes, may be less serious than the one just described, and may be about having the confidence to tell something to someone – for example, 'I want to tell Mummy that I am afraid of the dark', 'I want to tell my brother that I broke something of his', or 'I want to tell my teacher that I cannot understand what she is saying to me'.

The following example is a story that was told quite explicitly, and was causing a lot of distress for the child concerned. We used the ladder to create the stages, and then set up the scenes to role-play, a rung at a time. We started with the bottom rung and the top rung, the two extremes, and did a 'body sculpt' of each one, concentrating on how it felt to change from one situation to the other. We then created all the rungs or scenes in between. When we began to enact some scenes together, it was clear that the child had tried to tell several people about her worries but, so far, no one had listened. She was looking extremely pale and listless. She had tried to tell her mother about the noise, but her mother was always out; she had tried to tell the babysitter, but she was part of the noise; she had tried to tell her brother who had the noisy stereo, but he was the instigator of the noise. This is her ladder:

'This is how it is now'

This is how I would like it to be
I want to be able to sleep
If she still won't listen I will write her a note
I will try not to use the whiney voice which she hates
I will try and tell mummy at the weekend
I can't get to sleep at night because it is so noisy

After we had practised the stages of her ladder as part of the scenes of her story, she did feel empowered to try to talk to her mother again. She had already written a letter, just in case she did not have the opportunity to speak with her. However, they were able to sit down and talk. She also gave her mother the letter, and told me that her mother had decided that they should have an older babysitter, and not one who made just as much noise as her brother. (She also said that the mother was buying her brother a set of headphones!) It was a clear example of empowerment through dramatising the story.

The following is a sad tale, where the child felt burdened by, and responsible for, what was happening at home. It is clear that there needed to be some intervention, but also that the child and her siblings would need support during any changes that could be implemented.

'Once upon a time there was an angry fox who just kept on biting and biting. The baby foxes were very unhappy: they were losing their fur, and just stayed on their own and were very scared. The eldest cub was so unhappy because she could not look after the other cubs, and the angry fox said it was all her fault. What she really wanted was for the angry fox to stop being so angry or else ...' There was no more the girl could add to the story.

Together, we created her ladder, which, on the bottom rung, showed how the fox cub was feeling at present – 'The fox cub is very scared because the big fox is angry' – and on the top rung showed what the fox cub wished for: 'The fox cub wants a happy family.' We discussed the ladder and agreed that the four rungs in between meant: 'the fox cub needs to tell somebody how scared she is', 'the fox cub must remember she is only a cub', and 'the fox cub needs to stop blaming herself ', 'the fox cub needs someone to help her'. The final ladder is shown below.

The fox cub's ladder

The fox cub wants a happy family
The fox cub needs someone to help her
The fox cub needs to stop blaming herself
The fox cub must remember she is only a cub
The fox cub needs to tell somebody how scared she is
The fox cub is very scared because the big fox is angry

We can use the fox cub story with children who may be having a similar experience, making use of it to create insight and empathy – encourage the child to complete Worksheet 19. The outcome of this particular story is that the angry fox symbolised the father in a family of three children. His wife had left him, he had started to drink heavily and had more or less left the children to look after themselves. The child in question was the eldest, and felt responsible, blaming herself for the mother leaving. She was considered to look like her mother. The family did stay together, and there was a happier outcome through family support and therapeutic play.

Worksheet 19
The Fox Cub's Ladder

Name _____ Date _____

'The fox cub wants a happy family.'

'The fox cub needs someone to help her.'

'The fox cub needs to stop blaming herself.'

'The fox cub must remember she is only a cub.'

'The fox cub needs to tell someone how scared she is.'

'The fox cub is very scared because the big fox is angry.'

What do you think the child who wrote this story should do?

_____

_____

_____

_____

_____

_____

_____

Starters for Storytelling

There are many objects, cards, and props that we can use to start or structure a story, but we need to see them for what they are. They are props to facilitate the storytelling process, not the story in themselves. I have a range of the following objects and toys in my story room so that children, and indeed adults, can choose something to start or inspire a story, if they so wish.

Snowstorms and Sandstorms

Children delight in playing with snowstorm domes. I have a collection of 20 or more which can start many different stories. I have one set that presents depictions of fairy stories – 'Red Riding Hood', 'Hansel and Gretel', 'The Frog Prince' and 'The Little Mermaid'. Another set features monuments and statues from many places: Athens, San Francisco, Copenhagen, Dublin and Arundel. There are also nuns, winter scenes with snow, singers and skaters, and some contain a musical box as well. Remember that the water evaporates after a while! I usually suggest that the child shakes all of them up, and then makes a choice of one to tell a story, and then I do the same. We take it in turns to tell our stories, and can ask each other questions if we want. We can then make a drama from the story.

Children may like us to write their stories down, if they find writing difficult, and this text can be word-processed and returned to them. They may like to illustrate their printed stories, and then create an enactment.

Postcards and Pictures

Try to collect a diverse and evocative range of postcards. You can have a box of random cards, and you and the child can take turns to pick out a card to start a story. You can also have sets of cards that have themes. For example, I have lots of tree cards, a set showing doors and windows, and many cards showing ethnic dancers, artefacts and rituals. A diverse set of pictures of several generations of people can lead into family stories. I also have a set of cards that are all paintings of children that have proved to stimulate plenty of stories. There are also packs of cards for exploring feelings, difficulties, and situations which can create story structures. For example, the child can decide that the story should involve certain feelings, or that the story is about a particular difficulty. The cards help to create the characters, especially those packs that depict a range of feelings.

Managing the feelings of the character will assist us to manage our own feelings

Expressing the feelings of the character enables us to express our own feelings

The Prop Box

A wide range of props that do not belong to just one class or culture are invaluable for starting stories. You can include a necklace, a fan, a red-spotted handkerchief, a toothbrush, a pipe, a spanner, a phone, a wooden spoon, a large feather, a wallet or purse, a toy cockroach, sun-glasses, a mirror, a baby's bottle, a rain-rattle, an envelope with a foreign stamp – the list is almost endless! These props are objects that can appear in the story because they belong to a character, start off the action or are important to solve a mystery. You can begin a story-warm up by choosing a prop and then describing the person who owns it. You can then enact the person who owns this prop, and then create/enact their story.

You can also have a Magic Prop Box, which can contain a magic wand, a crystal stone, a small treasure box or bag, a pair of wings, a book of spells or a magic recipe book, coloured spectacles, a rose or lily, fossils, and so on. This box can take you into quite different sorts of roles and stories, and also help children to develop their imaginations. The Magic Prop Box can also empower a child to take control in situations where they feel helpless, and to create stories in which they can influence the outcome of events.

The Hat Box

We mentioned, earlier, the importance of having some dressing-up clothes, but it is also useful to have a Hat Box on its own. Collect and make as many different hats as you can: baseball caps, woolly caps, crowns and coronets, deer-stalker hats, bowler hats, flowery hats, top hats, trilby hats, cowboy hats, veils, uniform hats and caps, a chef's hat. The warm-up exercise can involve trying on the hat and introducing yourself, or walking around the room in that character. Then create a story that includes characters with some of the hats, and enact the story. You can develop the stories further by using the Prop Box and the Hat Box together to create characters and stories. Invite children to complete Worksheets 20 and 21, where they can think about various kinds of hat and design their own.

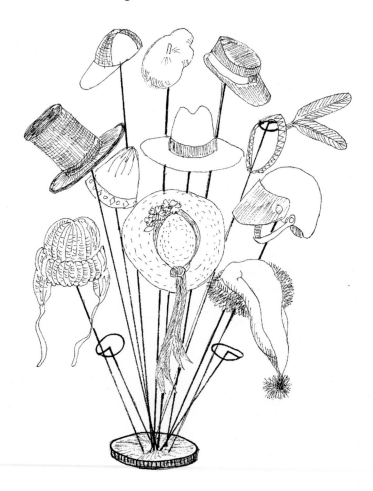

Worksheet 20
My Hat Box

Name _____ Date _____

Who are the people wearing these hats?

Worksheet 21
My Hat

Name _____ Date _____

Draw a hat that you would like to wear, and write about yourself wearing this hat. You might like to choose one from Worksheet 20, or you could design a new hat.

This is how I like to wear my hat!

_____

_____

_____

_____

_____

_____

The Story Tree

Just as we had the idea of the Story Cauldron or the Story pool, where we discovered stories, we can create the Story Box or the Story Tree. The idea is that there is always a container (such as a box, bag, or cauldron), or a piece of the landscape (such as a tree or a forest), where we can find stories to share.

Encourage children to draw a tree of their own that has been growing for a long, long time: it has deep roots and a strong trunk, and branches which may be bare, or with blossom or fruit. This is a tree about which there is a story, or it can even be the tree itself that is the character to tell a story.

For example, the story could have the tree as a central character: 'Once upon a time there was an old tree in the middle of the forest, and a wolf came to the tree for a meeting with the other wolves …' Or the tree can be a character, a wise witness to events: 'For many years the old tree in the woods had seen all the people who walked by. The tree had hundreds of stories stored in its roots, about people and animals, and their adventures and worries. One day the tree saw the young wolf come into the clearing and wondered …'

If the child is reluctant to draw his or her own tree, you can use one of the tree pictures on Story Sheet 13. We can also use the tree that we have used in other chapters as a story tree. Each apple can represent a story to be told, and the apples on the ground can be the good stories that have been forgotten.

Story Sheet 13a
The Story of My Tree (1)

Name _____ Date _____

The story of my tree is:

_____

_____

_____

_____

_____

_____

_____

Story Sheet 13b
The Story of My Tree (2)

Name _____ Date _____

The story of my tree is:

_____

_____

_____

_____

_____

_____

_____

Story Sheet 13c
The Story of My Tree (3)

Name _____ Date _____

The story of my tree is:

_____
_____
_____
_____
_____
_____
_____

168

Speechmark P This page may be photocopied for instructional use only. Creative Storytelling © Sue Jennings 2004

Creating Stories as Gifts

Sometimes we may need to tell a story for the child, and find a way for the child to be involved through illustrating the story. We need to be very careful not to impose a story with which the child has no connection: it may not necessarily be a story that is part of the child's life, as such, but it does need to have a connection through language or theme, and has to be appropriate to the child's age and culture. The following stories are fairly neutral, and provide an opportunity for the child to experience some potential support and hope. Story Sheets 14 and 15 follow, and are intended for the child to colour in and record their versions of the story.

The Magic Hula Bird

The magic Hula Bird lives in the old forest, and eats insects from the bark of old trees. The trees have grown very tall, and create lacy patterns against the sky. Many animals and birds make their homes in the old trees, including the Hula Bird. The magic Hula Bird has beautiful tail feathers of many bright colours, which sometimes float gently through the air and land on the forest floor. The Hula Bird knows when children are upset, and can sometimes give them a coloured feather to help them when they are upset. Children sometimes imagine that they are in the forest with their worries and fears, looking for a magic feather. A feather of the Hula Bird gives them something colourful to hold while the world is feeling very cloudy and grey.

The Dream Witch

Over the hills and far away on the top of a mountain lives a good witch. Her home is inside a rock cave, on the side of the mountain that faces towards the sea, and she sleeps soundly in the daytime as she listens to the soothing waves. She is a special witch who looks after children who do not have mummies and daddies to care for them. She sleeps in the daytime so that during the night she can visit all the homes where children need her. She travels on her broomstick, and circles around the roofs and sends the children beautiful dreams. So, if you lie quietly in bed and close your eyes, you can picture the Dream Witch scattering her dreams over the roof-tops, especially yours.'

Story Sheet 14
The Magic Hula Bird

Name _____ Date _____

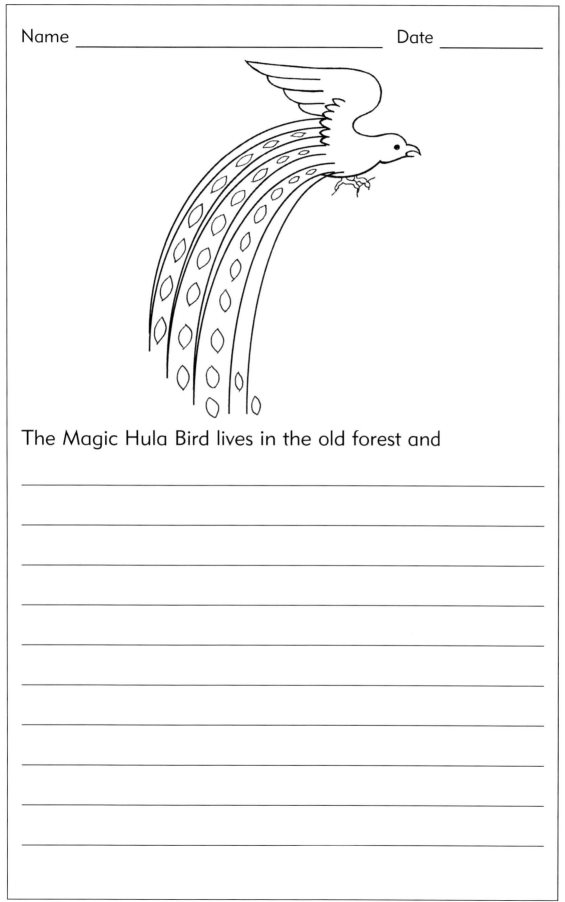

The Magic Hula Bird lives in the old forest and

_____

_____

_____

_____

_____

_____

_____

_____

_____

Story Sheet 15
The Dream Witch

Name _____ Date _____

I would like the Dream Witch to send me a dream story

about _____

_____

_____

_____

_____

_____

_____

The Closing Story

Rhiannon is an ancient Welsh goddess of the moon, and she rides on a beautiful white stallion. She is surrounded by flocks of birds as she beckons to the seasons in turn. Her horse never seems to be travelling very fast across the landscape, yet the hunters can never catch her. She is like the moon which does not seem to travel very fast, and yet we can never catch it.

And so it is that Rhiannon marries Prince Pwyll, who has been pursuing her for a long time. They have a son who is born on May Day and there is great rejoicing throughout the palace. However, tragedy strikes: the new born baby is kidnapped during the night and no one sees anything. Rhiannon's attendants are terrified that they might be accused of neglect, and blamed for the baby's disappearance. They decide to kill a puppy and smear the blood on Rhiannon in order to make it seem as if she has killed her own baby. Oh, what fear makes us do to innocent people!

For her punishment, Rhiannon has to go out and greet all visitors to the palace, and tell them the story of her wicked deed. Then she has to carry them on her back, as if they are on horseback, into the great hall of the palace. There, they are made welcome by the Prince and enjoy feasting and celebrating, from which, of course, Rhiannon is excluded.

This burden of punishment continues for many years and there is nothing that Rhiannon can do about it. Not only is she falsely accused of a very serious crime, she has also lost her new born baby and cannot be a mother to him. She continues to confess to the tale that is not true, and carries young and old alike on her back

One day a farmer comes to the palace with a strange question. As Rhiannon goes to tell the story and carry him on her back, he asks her to wait a moment since there is something he wants to ask her. Rhiannon cannot imagine that he can want to talk to her, especially when he has heard the story, but he insists:

'Are you the mother who lost a child some three years past? Are you the woman who has mourned a babe that disappeared in the night?'

Rhiannon bursts into tears as the Prince comes striding out of the palace to demand why she is not carrying the farmer into the great hall. The farmer interrupts the Prince's shouting and tells him that he and his wife have been caring for an abandoned child for several years. The baby had been stolen in the night by a wicked demon, who then went to the farm to steal a fine horse to ride home on. The farmer chased the demon off his farm, and he dropped the baby in his hurry to get away.

The farmer and his wife, being childless, decide to keep the child and bring him up as their own. Only now have they heard the story of the loss of Rhiannon's baby, and have come to see if it is true. The farmer rushes home and comes back with his wife who is carrying the young boy, and Rhiannon clasps him close. The family is at last reunited. Rhiannon tell the farmer and his wife that they can continue to visit the boy and behave like family towards him.

There is a feasting and a celebrating to welcome the young Prince home, and to place Rhiannon in her rightful place in the palace. Prince Pwyll asks her forgiveness for having believed that she could commit such a terrible deed. The servants who told the lies have already run away, never to be seen again. And peace reigns at the palace once more.

As years go by, Rhiannon is more and more revered as a woman of wisdom, who can be especially helpful to women having babies. Her story reminds us of the pain of false accusation, and reminds us never to pre-judge a situation, especially through prejudice.

> Rhiannon – give me the wisdom
> to let go of the past,
> strengthen the present,
> and illuminate the future.

CHAPTER 11

Resources

T HE AVAILABILITY OF INFORMATION for play therapists and play workers is growing all the time and the following addresses have useful information. It is not an exhaustive list and more can be gained by searching on the internet.

Training Courses: Play Therapy and Related Training Programmes in the UK

Postgraduate Certificate, Diploma, MA

Institute for Arts and Therapy in Education
2–18 Britannia Row
Islington
London
N1 8PA
+44 (0) 207 704 2534

Liverpool Hope College
Hope Park
Liverpool
L16 9JD
+44 (0) 161 291 3161

Notre Dame Centre *(in association with University of Strathclyde)*
20 Athole Gardens
Glasgow
G12 9BA
+44 (0) 141 339 2366

Play Therapy UK *(in association with University of Chichester)*
Fern Hill Centre
Fairwarp
E Sussex
TN22 3BU
+44 (0) 1825 712312

Playtime *(in association with Leeds Metropolitan University)*
6 The Green
Roade
Northamptonshire
NN7 2PD
+44 (0) 1604 861947

University of Roehampton *(Surrey)*
Southlands College
80 Roehampton Lane
London
SW15 5SL
+44 (0) 208 392 3709

University of York
Department of Social Policy and Social Work
Heslington
York
YO10 5DD
+44 (0)1904 432

Short Courses are run in the UK by most of the above organisations and in addition:

Action Work *(Regional, International)*
1 The Sycamores
Celtic Way
Bleadon
Somerset
BS24 0NF
+44 07815 855672

Anna Freud Centre *(London)*
21 Maresfield Gardens
London
NW3 5SD
+44 (0) 207 794 2313

Common Threads *(Hampshire and Regional)*
Wessex House
Upper Market Street
Eastleigh
Hampshire
SC50 9FD
+44 (0) 7000 785215

Family Futures Consortium *(London and National)*
35 Britannia Road
Islington
London
N1 8QH
+44 (0) 207 354 4161

Jenny Mosley Consultancy *(Wiltshire and Regional)*
28A, Gloucester Road
Trowbridge
Wiltshire
BA14 0AA
+44 (0) 1225 719204

Nexus *(London and Regional)*
Suites 10 & 11, Kent House
87 Regent Street
London
W1B 4EH
+44 (0)207 439 7700 or (0)1483 306125

Quality Training UK *(Regional)*
Marily House
Bowling Green Lane
Honiton
Devon
EX14 2DP
+44 (0) 1404 46233

Rowan Studio *(Glastonbury, National and International)*
PO Box 3567
Glastonbury
Somerset
BA6 8ZR
+44 (0) 458 830434

Sprito *(Regional)*
PO Box 4858
Earley
Reading
RG5 4TP
+44 (0) 207 388 7755

Tavistock Centre *(London and National)*
120 Belsize Lane
London
NW3 5BA
+44 (0) 207 447 3786

Young Minds *(London and Regional)*
102–108 Clerkenwell Road
Farringdon
London
EC1M 5SA
+44 (0) 207 336 8445

Relevant Associations and Organisations

Action Work
1 The Sycamores
Celtic Way
Bleadon
Somerset
BS24 0NF

+44 07815 855672   info@actionwork.com
www.actionwork.com   www.bully.org

Film, theatre and training for schools and the community. Current specialist areas: bullying, racism, drug misuse, young people' relationships.

British Association of Play Therapists
31 Cedar Drive
Keynsham
Bristol
BS31 2TY

01179 860390   info@bapt.uk.com
www.bapt.uk.com

Full, associate and student membership. Newsletter *Play Therapy*, journal *British Journal of Play Therapy*. Conferences and seminars. Regional support groups.

Children's Play Council
8 Wakely Street
london
ECIV 7QE

+44 (0) 207 843 6016
www.ncb.org.uk

Part of the National Children's Bureau, promoting the interests and well-being of children and young people across every aspect of their lives.

Common Threads
Wessex House
Upper Market Street
Eastleigh
Hampshire
SO50 9FD

+44 (0) 7000 785 215   info@commonthreads.co.uk

Short courses 'Playwork', bi-monthly publication *Play Words*, books and training packs.

Institute for Arts in Therapy and Education
2–18 Britannia Row
Islington
London
N1 8PA

+44 (0) 207 704 2534

Training in integrative child psychotherapy and supervision.

Institute of Reflective Practice
Overton Business Centre
Maisemore
Gloucestershire
GL2 8HR

+44 (0) 1452 309897
www.reflectivepractices.com

Jenny Mosley Consultancy
28A Gloucester Road
Trowbridge
Wiltshire
BA14 0AA

+44 (0) 1225 719204
positivepress@jennymosley.co.uk
www.circle-time.co.uk

Training courses and workshops: 'circle time', 'clapping games' Publications:
Positive Press Ltd, 'Golden Rule books' and many more.

Playlink
Unit 5
11 Mowll Street
London
SW9 6BG

+44 (0)207 820 3800   info@playlink.org
www.playlink.org

Information and publications.

Play Therapy International (PTI)
Fern Hill Centre
Fairwarp
East Sussex
TN22 3BU

+44 (0) 1825 712312   ptiorg@aol.com

International body for play therapists and child psychotherapists, promotes affiliated organisations within regional cultural context: Play Therapy UK established in 1999, Play Therapy Ireland in 2003 and Play Therapy Romania in 2004. Provides certification of courses and practitioners and publishes 'Play for Life' a quarterly journal for practitioners. Conferences and networking events.

Play Therapy UK – The United Kingdom Society for Play and Creative Arts
Therapies
Fern Hill Centre
Fairwarp
East Sussex
TN22 3BU

+44 (0)1825 712312   ptukorg@aol.com
www.playtherapy.org

Membership open to those who use therapeutic play in their work and play therapists. Training courses at all levels validated internally on IBECPT standards, and externally by University of Chichester. Manages SEPACTO, a database of clinical outcomes that shows the effectiveness of play therapy interventions.

Playtime: Play Therapy Services Northamptonshire
6 The Green
Roade
Northamptonshire
NN7 2PD

Training, staff development, job creation

Play Wales
Baltic house
Mount Stuart Square
Cardiff
CF10 5FH

+44 (0) 292 048 6050 mail@playwales.org.uk
www.playwales.org.uk

Rowan Studio
PO Box 3567
Glastonbury
BA6 8ZR

+44 (0) 1458 830434   drsuejennings@hotmail.com
www.suejennings.com   www.rowanromania.com

International and national training and advisory service, play training programme in Romania, and overseas volunteers through PTRo, peace workshops, team building. Book service and publications. Internet resource for people working with children.

Society for Storytelling
PO Box 2344
Reading
RG6 7PG

+44 (0) 01752 569244   sfs@fairbruk.demon.co.uk

Worshops, newsletter, very active email news.

SPRITO Playwork Unit
The Playwork Unit Skills Active
Castlewood House
77–91 New Oxford Street
London
WC1A 1PX

+44 (0) 207 388 7755
www.playwork.org.uk

National Network for Playwork Education and Training. Centres in: North East, North West, Yorkshire and the Humber, East Midlands, West Midlands, East and South East, South West. Taking forward DCMS funded by National Strategy for Training and Education 'Quality Training, Quality Play'.

Winston's Wish
The Clara Burgess Centre
Gloucestershire Royal Hospital
Great Western Road
Gloucester
GL1 3NN

+44(0) 1452 394377   info@winstonswish.org.uk
www.winstonswish.org.uk

Supporting bereaved children and young people.

CHAPTER 12

Bibliography

References and Further Reading

Axline V, 1964, *Dibs in Search of Self,* Penguin, London.

Axline V, 1947/1969, *Play Therapy,* Ballantine, New York.

Bannister A & Huntington A, 2002, *Communicating with Children and Adolescents: Action for Change,* Jessica Kingsley, London.

Berg O, 1998, personal communication, OEMP Conference, Copenhagen, Denmark.

Brooking-Payne K, 1996, *Games Children Play,* Hawthorn Press, Stroud.

Carson R, 1965, *Silent Spring,* Penguin, Harmondsworth.

Cattanch A, 1992, *Play Therapy with Abused Children,* Jessica Kingsley, London.

Cattanach A, 1994, *Play Therapy: Where the Sky Meets the Underworld,* Jessica Kingsley, London.

Cattanach A, 1997, *Children's Stories in Play Therapy,* Jessica Kingsley, London.

Cattanach A, Chesner S, Jennings S, Mitchell S & Meldrum B, 1994, *The Handbook of Dramatherapy,* Routledge, London.

Cattanach A, Chesner S, Jennings S, Mitchell S & Meldrum B, (ed), 1995, *Dramatherapy with Children and Adolescents,* Routledge, London.

Evans R, 2000, *Helping Children to overcome fear: the healing power of play,* Hawthorn, Stroud.

Courtney R & Schattner G, 1982, *Drama in Therapy: Volume 1 Children,* Drama Book Specialists, New York.

Garhard Mooney C, 2000, *Theories of Childhood,* Redleaf Press, Minnesota.

Gersie A & King N, 1990, *Storymaking in Education and Therapy,* Jessica Kingsley, London.

Gersie A, 1991, *Storymaking in Bereavement,* Jessica Kingsley, London.

Gersie A, 1992, *Earth Tales,* Green Press, London.

Hansen T, 1991, *Seven for a Secret: Healing the wounds of sexual abuse in childhood,* SPCK, London.

Hickson A, 1995, *Creative Action Methods in Groupwork,* Speechmark, Bicester.

Horley E, 1998, 'Developmental Assessment of Play' presented to OEMP Conference, Copenhagen, Denmark.

Jennings S, 1973/2004, *Remedial Drama,* A & C Black/Play Therapy Press.

Jennings S, (ed), 1975, *Creative Therapy,* Pitman/Kemble Press, Banbury.

Jennings S, 1979, 'Ritual and the Learning Process', *Journal of Dramatherapy,* 13.4.

Jennings S, 1986 *Creative Drama in Groupwork,* Speechmark, Bicester.

Jennings S, (ed), 1987 *Dramatherapy Theory and Practice,* Vol 1, 2, 3, Routledge, London.

Jennings S, 1990, *Dramatherapy with Families, Groups and Individuals,* Jessica Kingsley, London.

Jennings S & Minde A, 1993, *Art Therapy and Dramatherapy: Masks of the Soul,* Jessica Kingsley, London.

Jennings S, 1993/2004, *Playtherapy with Children: A Practitioners Guide,* Blackwell/Play Therapy Press Fairwarp.

Jennings S, 1998, *Introduction to Dramatherapy: Ariadne's Ball of Thread,* Jessica Kingsley, London.

Jennings S, 1997, *Introduction to Developmental Playtherapy,* Jessica Kingsley, London.

Jennings S, 2000, *Brigid: Fertility, creativity and healing,* Rowan Studio, Glastonbury.

Jennings S, 2001, *Inanna: Journey into darkness and light,* Rowan Studio, Glastonbury.

Jennings S, 2001, *Embodiment – Project – Role* training video, Actionwork, Bleadon.

Jennings S & Hickson A, 2002, 'Pause for Thought: Action or Stillness with Young People' in *Communicating with Children and Adolescents,* eds Bannister A & Huntingdon A, Jessica Kingsley, London.

Jennings S, 2003, 'EPR – A Model for Dramatic Play', in *Play Words,* April/May.

Jennings S, 2003, 'Playlore: the roots of humanity', in *Play for Life,* Autumn.

Jennings S, 2003, 'Playlore: The Sensory Foundation', in *The Prompt Winter,* 2003/2004.

Jennings S, 2004, 'Playtherapy in Romania' in *Play Words,* February/March.

Jennings S, 2004, 'Social Play and Inclusion' in *Play Words,* May/June.

Jennings S, 2004, Embodiment–Projection–Role with Children, training video Actionwork, Bleadon.

Jennings S, 2004, *Goddesses: Ancient Wisdom in Times of Change,* Chrysalis, London.

John M, 2001, *Children's Rights and Power,* Jessica Kingsley, London.

Lahad M, 1992, '*Story-making and assessment method for coping with stress',* in *Dramatherapy: Theory and Practice,* Vol 2, Jennings S (ed), Tavistock/Routledge, London.

Lahad M, 2000, Creative Supervision, Jessica Kingsley, London.

Lowenfeld M, 1935, *Play in Childhood,* Mackeith Press, London.

Mellon N, 2000, *Storytelling with Children,* Hawthorn Press, Stroud.

Miller A, 1990, *The Untouched Key,* Virago Press, London.

Miller A, 1983, *For Your Own Good,* Faber, London.

Meyer R, 2001, *The Wisdom of Fairy Tales,* Floris Books, Edinburgh.

Oaklander V, 1978, *Windows to our Children,* Real People Press, Utah.

Sherborne V, 2001, *Developmental Movement for Children,* Worth Reading, London.

Slade P, 1954, *Child Drama,* Hodder and Stoughton, London.

Slade P, 1995, *Child Play: its importance for human development,* Jessica Kingsley, London.

Spolin V, 1963, *Improvisation for the New Theater,* North Western University Press, Everston.

Sunderland M, 2000, *Using Story Telling as a Therapeutic Tool with Children,* Speechmark, Bicester.

Vygotsky L, 1978, *Mind in Society,* Edited by Michael Cole, Harvard University Press, Cambridge MA.

Winnicott D, 1974, *Playing and Reality,* Pelican, London.

Books for Children

THERE ARE MANY BOOKS for children that assist them in addressing different issues in their lives through the power of the story, themes, roles and metaphors. They can also be useful when planning work and inspiration is needed. The following is a small selection of useful titles.

Baxter N, 1998, *Fairy Tales from Hans Christian Anderson*, Armadillo, Leicester.

Baxter N, 1999, *Oscar Wilde Stories for Children*, Armadillo, Leicester.

Brothers Grimm, 1975, *The Complete Grimm's Fairy Tales*, RKP, London.

Corrin S & Corrin S, 1984, *Stories for Seven-Year-Olds*, Puffin, London.

Elsie R (trans), 2001, *Albanian Folktales and Legends*, Dukagjini Printing, Kosovo.

Friedlander G, 2001, *Jewish Fairy Tales*, New York, Dover Publications.

Holaday D, **Chin Woon Ping & Teoh Boon Seong**, 2003, *Bes Hyang Dney and other Jah Hut Stories*, Center for Orang Asli Concerns, Malaysia.

Landy RL, 2001, *God Lives in Glass: Reflections of God through the eyes of Children***,** Skylight Paths Publishing, Woodstock.

O'Neill C, Casterton P & Headlam C, (eds), 1998, *The Kingfisher Book of Mythology: Gods, Goddesses and Heroes from around the World*, Kingfisher, London.

Opie I & Opie P, 1975, *The Classic Fairy Tales*, Book Club Associates, London.

Rosen M (ed), 1992, *South and North, East and West: The Oxfam Book of Children's Stories*, Walker Books, London.

Practical Resources for Working with Children

Toys and equipment are easily obtainable from educational suppliers and have the advantage that they will all have been tested for safety and toxicity. However, local charity shops and car boot sales also yield useful finds. Try to avoid stereotyped toys that leave little room for the imagination and include as many 'natural materials', especially wood, as possible.

The following packs and manuals are excellent resources for story and play work:

ColorCards series, colour photographic flashcards including *Emotions* for working with feelings and as a stimulus for role play, Speechmark, Bicester.

Creative Activities in Groupwork series, titles include *Creative Drama in Groupwork*, *Creative Writing in Groupwork*, *Creative Art in Groupwork*, *CreativeGames in Groupwork*. Practical workbooks with techniques and applications. Especially useful is *Creative Action Methods in Groupwork*, with many ideas for work with children and adolescents, Speechmark, Bicester.

Developing Strengths series including 'feeling spectrum', 'cognitive spectrum' 'social scenes', 'story scenes'. Written by Sue Jennings, published by Rowan Studio, Glastonbury.

Feeling Elf Cards and Games, Elizabeth Crary & Peaco Todd. A card set of feelings with words in English, Spanish and Japanese with a cheeky elf illustrating the expression and the posture, Parenting Press Inc, Seattle.

Group Games series, titles include: *Group Games: Social Skills*, *Group Games: Dealing with Aggression*, *Group Games: Emotional Strength & Self-Esteem*, Excellent practical ideas, Speechmark, Bicester.

Helping Children with Feelings series by Margot Sunderland and Nicky Armstrong. Practical work books which include a story book for the child. Titles include *Helping Children with Loss*, *Helping Children with Fear*, *Helping Children with Low Self-Esteem*, Speechmark, Bicester.

Storycards series by Sue Duggleby & Ross Duggleby – picture cards for language development and stories, titles include *Prepositions* and *Adjectives*, Speechmark, Bicester.

Books on themes for special situations

Asher J, 2003, *Moppy is Happy,* Positive Press, Trowbridge.
Illustrated by Gerald Scarfe, this book forms part of a set to assist children in understanding and dealing with their emotions. Moppy turns bright yellow with happiness, when he is accepted by his new friend. In *Moppy is Angry* he turns bright red with anger when he feels he is being ignored.

Browne A , 1991, *Willy and Hugh,* Random House, London.
Willy is lonely and doesn't have any friends – until he meets Hugh – and a close friendship forms between two very different creatures.

Chichester Clark E, 2001, *I Love You Blue Kangaroo*, Collins, London.
A delightful tale of Lily and her toy kangaroo who gets forgotten and found again (the kangaroo is supplanted by lots of other toys until found). Also by the same author *Where Are You Blue Kangaroo?* and *It Was You, Blue Kangaroo!*

Crossley D, 2000, *Muddles, Puddles and Sunshine: Your activity book to help when someone has died,* Hawthorn Press, Gloucester.

Sendak M, 2000, *Where the Wild Things Are,* Red Fox/Random House, London.
When Max is sent to his room he creates a forest and sails to the home of the wild things who make him their king – and then the rumpus starts! He sails home feeling very lonely and finds that his supper is in his room.

Turner M, 1988, *Talking with Children and Young People about Death and Dying,* Jessica Kingsley, London.